Walking Barefoot in my Shoes

By Doreen Brust Johnson

Walking Barefoot in my Shoes

Photos provided by the author
Book design by Jansina of Rivershore Books

ISBN: 978-1-63522-001-8

Printed in the United States of America
10   9   8   7   6   5   4   3   2

RIVERSHORE   BOOKS

Rivershore Books
8982 Van Buren St. NE • Minneapolis, MN 55434
763-670-8677 • info@rivershorebooks.com

Dedication

This story is dedicated to . . .

My mother Elsa (Emma) for your bravery to move forward at a time when this was virtually un-heard of in order that Edwin (Fritz) and I (Katrin) may have a better life away from the harsh barren prairies. You took a lot of criticism, but never gave up on what you felt was best even if at times your path was not always the best choice.

As we all look back on our lives we see where our paths have not been the best either. We carry on trying to make tomorrow a better day just as you did.

While it was bitter sweet for Edwin and I, we owe you a world of gratitude. We were given the opportunity to choose our own paths. Without saying I felt you were torn knowing we would be leaving the father we loved for an education as we left the brink of starvation behind.

Your inspiration gave me the strength to write your story of courage and caring. To stand alone on what you believed was necessary while many were critical of your choice just because you were a woman making your own decisions. In spite of your mistakes you were a very brave woman, few could have done what you felt compelled to do. You showed me how to be strong as I too faced some hard decisions, of a different kind, travelling along life's path. You taught us what it is like to work hard for the necessities of life.

To my Friends and Readers

Thank you for your dedication and loyalty as you followed my books as they made their journey through the publishing process. I am so very grateful for your support. Your viewing, sharing and liking my posts helped to make this long journey fun and exciting.

Momma, Momma, the Preachers' Comin has brought to me memories of both happy and sad times. I thank each of you for sharing with me your feelings of the choices made by Emma and Floyd. May this sequel bring both answers and understanding to your questions.

My wish is that they bring to each of you some quiet reading time, and perhaps rekindle some fond memories of experiences shared by you and your family. I am sure there will also be some memories brought back of tough times where tears were shed and nerves were frayed. That is a part of life's journey that we all must go through. Focus on the good. Share often with the younger generation so they may know you better. Do not keep your past life to yourself as I have done. Yes, I too have been criticized for the choices of my parents. Now I know and believe that it was not my fault, and so I feel free to talk about the past. Let these experiences make you stronger as they have done to me. Without them I do not know who I would be today.

I pass to each of you God's richest blessings as you continue walking life's path.

Best Wishes,

Doreen

In Remembrance of Mother

Katrin standing in our yard beside the bomb shelter (the black circle is the lid to the entrance below ground).

This is where we lived upon arrival to the city. Our bachelor suite was upstairs with a small balcony.

Emma in her backyard in the city.

Visiting Stanley Park on Mother's Day in 1952
Katrin standing – Nancy standing; Mother sitting;
Fritz sitting in the front

Fritz (Edwin) –Floyd (Dad) –Katrin (Doreen)
On the farm in Carrot River, Saskatchewan

Prologue

As I sit in my comfortable blue rocking chair gazing out the living room window at the calm deep blue waters of the ocean, I find myself thinking of my life today. Never did I think that I would have such a beautiful apartment, ever so comfortable and warm, decorated just the way I like it. It is not elaborate, but everything that I need is here.

My children, Fritz and Katrin along with their families are within visiting distance. That is what I am most grateful for. Joe and Katrin live the closest. They bring my grandchildren, Dawn and Bruce with them. I always have cookies and cream soda pop for them.

Today I am going to meet three lady friends for lunch. We like to have fish and chips at Moby Dick's Restaurant, our favourite place to dine at our favourite table set and waiting for us to arrive each Tuesday at noon. They also have a take-out window which is extremely popular. Their prices are reasonable, the service friendly, the portions huge, the atmosphere quaint. As we sit lingering over our coffee we watch the seagulls flying low hoping to find pieces of deep fried fish waiting for them.

I am easily reminded of the hard life we shared in Northern Saskatchewan. While it is tucked safely in my memory, it is never too far away to reminisce.

Chapter One

As the train slowly crept into Medicine Hat, Alberta stopping beside the platform leaving it's dirty smoke behind, I frantically scanned the station for a sign of my sister Ursula and her husband Otto. Just as I was beginning to panic that maybe they will be late, I saw Ursula with her friendly smile lighting up her face as she began to wave to us. She looked just like I remembered her only prettier. It has been much too long since I have seen her.

I hurried my children off so I could now begin this new life. One that I was sure was to be better for them. I knew from the beginning of this that it was not going to be easy. I also knew that we would make it. We had to.

After many hugs and kisses covered with happy tears, Otto led us to his vehicle. A beautiful dark blue car with a heater inside. The children and I sat in the back, them enjoying the sights of the big city. I could only look at Ursula. I can't even remember how many years it has been since we saw each other. Being older than myself, she had left home many years before me. When I was little she was like a second mother to me. I cried so hard when she had to leave to find work somewhere else. I wanted her to come home to sleep at night. Oh for the comprehension of a small child.

After arriving at their beautiful large stucco home Ursula and I spent the next few hours talking of a little bit of everything and a lot of nothing. We just wanted to be together where we felt we would never again have to say goodbye.

Soon it was time to help with dinner. A delicious dinner was waiting for her family and us in the oven. I was so excited I can't remember what we ate. I do remember it being so scrumptious. There was so much food on the table I felt like we were at a banquet in the fanciest hotel. Today Ursula prepared a special Sunday dinner just for us.

That evening we spent together getting to know each other once again. Her four children were older than mine, but they easily talked to Fritz and Katrin. Fritz was just too happy to tell of their escapades on the train while Katrin was too shy to enter into the conversation. I had no idea of the things they did. To think how easily they could have fallen off the platform between the train cars as they hung over the edge to watch the wheels speeding along.

When it was time for them to go to bed, Ursula and I took them to the basement where three more beautiful bedrooms waited. Each one furnished with a bed and matching dresser. A curtain matched the pretty thick quilt that lay on top of a fresh white sheet covering a comfortable mattress. A hand embroidered pillowcase covered a fluffy pillow for each. Each room was in a different colour. There was only one big problem.

They had never been so far apart. I showed them all the rooms, how close they would still be, but still the tears began to flow. This was too far for them. After Ursula and I thought we had them settled we went upstairs for more visiting. So much to share.

Some hours later after having talked well into the night, I decided to check on the children before retiring. To no surprise, Katrin's bed was empty. This would take them some time to adjust.

With touring the city and visiting Otto's relatives the days passed quickly. Christmas was fast approaching and once again I had no money for gifts for anyone. Every time my children were asked what they wanted from Santa they said nothing. They did not know what to wish for so they never asked for anything. No one had ever before asked them what they wanted. I had never dared to as I knew we could not give it to them. I was grateful to Mrs. Faust for making it possible to give them each a popcorn ball.

Three weeks passed since we arrived. Fritz and Katrin enjoyed riding their bicycles most every day up and down the smooth sidewalks. I have no idea how far they went, but I am sure it was further than the boundary I had set.

Sunday afternoons we went along with Otto and Ursula for a drive to check out their oil well that stood tall in their country property. I was so fascinated watching the giant arm slowly moving up and down that would supposedly bring oil up from far down into the earth. I found this very difficult to imagine let alone believe. We had stones and roots, they had oil. While Otto tried to explain this to Fritz and Katrin they just could not comprehend. They had never heard of oil coming from the ground.

Another favourite drive was to Drumheller, Alberta, the Dinosaur Capital of the World, to view the amazing erosion formations where the dinosaurs had roamed many thousands of years earlier. The hoodoos are natural vertical structures of soft sandstone leaving a feeling of having been deserted for thousands of years along with the dinosaurs. Faces of the Native forefathers were etched in the solid rock in shades of brown and rust in the slick surface.

It was difficult for Fritz and Katrin to be interested as they had never heard of a dinosaur. To me this was fascinating. These hills were as barren as compared to the hills of Qu'Appelle Valley in Saskatchewan that we had seen on our trip with the Faust family to visit my sister Rose. There the rolling hills that stretched for miles were covered in a lush green mixture of wild grass with healthy bushes scattered throughout the Valley further than the eye could see. But they had not had dinosaurs living there.

Before I knew it Christmas arrived. Ursula and Otto had been assuring me that I was not to worry about presents. They had some for both Katrin and Fritz. There was even a beautiful warm sweater in a rich rose colour for me. I was overcome. I had not received a Christmas present since I had left home where our mother was sure to have a fresh white handkerchief that she had embroidered in pretty soft colours for each of us girls.

Christmas dinner was a feast to behold. The turkey in the oven was roasted to a golden brown filled with a dressing that tasted just like what our mother had made. This came with all the trimmings my children had never had. They had never tasted cranberry sauce or plum pudding with rich hard sauce that carried a faint taste of rum. Oh my. Even though I was so full from this elaborate dinner I just had to have pudding and sauce.

When the dishes were cleaned and put away, we made ourselves comfortable in the living room with the soft sounds of Christmas Carols in the background. It seemed it was only minutes later that Otto brought out a basket of a mixture of nuts in their shells. They had only ever seen and eaten peanuts. Ever so patiently Otto shelled each different kind explaining what they were as they tasted them over and over again.

Just when I thought they had eaten enough to last for at least three days, Otto got up and went out. Now I wondered just where he was going at this time of the evening, but since Ursula showed no sign of curiosity I pushed it aside.

Otto came back in shortly carrying a large pretty tin about twelve inches square. Without saying a word he quietly walked over to his chair and sat down. Ursula began to smile. She knew.

"Katrin. Come see what Uncle has."

Without moving she looked at Fritz which brought him to his feet. They slowly walked over standing beside Otto. Gently he took Fritz by the hand and drew him to his other side. "There now, you both can see."

"What is it Uncle?" asked Fritz.

"It is a special Christmas treat called Halvah that is made in Jerusalem. It is basically a mixture of sesame seeds, butter and honey. If you eat too much at one time, you will get a tummy ache so we will have a little each evening. Is that ok?"

"Yes Uncle," they both said followed by a polite thank you. I was so proud of how they remembered to use their manners without being prodded.

The next day after another big dinner of leftovers that tasted just as good, Ursula brought out a fancy cake plate that was piled high with Ginger Nut cookies. Made from our mother's delicious recipe. They filled me with so many memories of home it brought tears to my eyes. Dear Ursula had made all the special treats from home for us to enjoy together. This was truly a Christmas to remember.

As we all sat around in the living room Otto began to speak of the train ride as he relaxed on his big soft arm chair covered in plush brown corduroy. Ursula and I sat on a beautiful soft flowered sofa with round decorator cushions she had made. Fritz and Katrin seemed to bounce between us and the floor not really knowing just where they wanted to be.

His comments did not seem to gain any participation from either of the children so he took a more direct approach.

"I think I will bring in the Halvah and then you can tell Uncle how much fun you had riding the train and what all you did. Ya?"

This time I had to prompt them to answer. Reluctantly they both said yes as they looked at each other. Now what else had they been up to? If Otto thought they would tell on each other he was in for a surprise. I sat back not saying anything leaving this conversation for him to handle. I knew them better than he did. There is no way they will tell their secrets, at least not intentionally.

For a while I thought they were most fascinated with the speed of the train as it passed the trees taking us on to new sights. Then Otto began to ask specific questions.

"Tell Uncle about it. Did you have to spend all the time sitting on that hard cold seat?"

"No. We ran back and forth in the car because there was no where to go. We went outside and stood on the platform for a while watching the wheels turning faster and faster leaving a huge round stream of grey smoke behind.

Sometimes we saw men jump on and climb up to the roof. They always motioned for us to be quiet and not say anything. One man said they were going to lay on top of the cars and look at the stars all night, but don't tell anyone. We didn't really think they did.

Sometimes we talked to the conductor. He asked us where we were going and how come we weren't going to school. Sometimes he told us to go sit down with our mother so we wouldn't disturb the other people. So we did. We played hide and seek hiding in the cupboards above the seats. No one looked for us except the conductor. When it got dark we could see the coyotes watching the train go by. The wheels were noisy. It felt like it was going over bumps. That is all we did." I did not add that I had seen a kind lady sitting near the door handing them each a cookie on more than one occasion. Whenever I needed to use the washroom, I discreetly said "Thank you" to this generous lady. She just smiled saying not a word.

Otto gave Ursula that look that said he would talk to them. She and I went to the kitchen to do something that didn't need to be done. Now I knew I had another worry until we got to Martha's. There is no way that two children accustomed to being active and outdoors would be able to sit on a seat all day. I loved to look out the window, but I am an adult. We like to do those things. They like to climb trees.

Chapter Two

Once again it was time to get the train for our ride on the next leg of our journey. I would see Martha. This time it would just be a long day. We would not need to spend the night sleeping on the cold hard seats sitting up with no blanket to cover us leaving us to wake feeling a chill.

As I packed our belongings once more I felt a sadness at having to leave Ursula not knowing if once again it would be a long time before we would be able to visit together, perhaps never. The children were just feeling at home there. They enjoyed all the extra treats Otto gave them like ice cream cones just before dinner. Chocolate bars on Sunday afternoons. It seemed he needed to slip over to their bakery for something he had forgotten to do before leaving for the day taking them with him. This also seemed to give him an appetite for ice cream. I knew that when we were on our own again there would be no more treats so I let it go making little fuss over the uneaten dinners. Ursula would pretend to scold him, but I knew by the smile as she turned her back that it was just for show. She was still as tender hearted as I remembered.

I went to bed feeling a little sad that I had not been truthful with Fritz and Katrin as to where we were now going. They thought they would be seeing their dad soon. Instead I told them how we were going a little further to visit another Aunty. Again we would go on the train this time taking us to warmer weather and the city. Rose told me how she had told so many stories to her children during her difficult times, she was afraid she would never be able to forgive herself. I am now beginning to find myself doing the same.

Morning came early. The stars had returned to the cover of the night sky that had not left us when I went down stairs to wake Fritz and Katrin. Ursula and I had spent a few minutes together over our morning coffee discussing what may lie ahead. She wanted to assure me that her and Otto would be willing to help me along. Otto had stressed that we must not return to the farm. It was unfortunately one that did not have good rich soil for growing crops no matter how hard we worked. There was sure to be work that Floyd would be able to do if only he was just willing. I knew he loved his children more than anyone or anything in the world. He would not be willing to give them up nor was he able to provide for them. His pride was standing in his way.

Before going to bed, they both said good bye to Max, Ursula's fluffy white Pomeranian that could be found sleeping peacefully on her feet anytime she sat down. I knew Fritz was missing his toffee coloured collie Butch even though he never mentioned it. Floyd would look after him. They would be company for each other.

As we boarded the train they seemed both excited and sad. Excited for what lay ahead, but sad for what was left behind. With all that was on my mind as to how I would cope with the future, I could not even begin to assure them all would be well because I did not know. I just knew that I had to try. If Rose could do what she did, then surely I could do this for my children.

This time as the steam locomotive rattled along, we had warmer clothes. Ursula had given Katrin a red coat with a fur collar from one of her daughters that had outgrown it some years earlier. Fritz inherited a new suit from her son with a matching tweed cap. This time they did not look like the poorest farmer's young ones.

Our sandwiches were made with fresh bread from their bakery filled with homemade summer sausage and homemade German mustard that tasted just like Mother had made when we were young. At least it was the way I remembered it. There were plenty of cookies for our treats after our meals that had been carefully wrapped in wax paper to stay fresh.

As we left the warmth of their cozy home I felt the wind had come up this morning with a bit more of a bite to it. While there was snow covering the ground, it was a very small amount compared to the three feet that we had been used to having at this time of year. The wind would not be able to wrap itself around our bodies chilling us through to our bones. For all of this I was grateful.

This time our ride on the train was different. It still had the chugging sounds of the wheels rolling along as it huffed and puffed leaving the dark smell of the steam lingering behind. There was not an empty seat to be seen. No one got on or off all day long. The conductor stopped to remind me every once in a while as he walked past that my children would need to remain in their seats. No walking back and forth in the car except to use the washroom he could be heard saying in his stern voice as he passed by the passengers. I knew this was going to be a long day and evening.

This conductor was different from the previous one. He frequently made a point of stopping by us to ask why a woman with two children would be travelling alone. I told him how we were going to visit my sister for a while. I have a feeling I was a poor liar. Maybe my conscience was bothering me, but I didn't think he believed me. That part was true. Sometimes he seemed to be more interested in Floyd than us. It seemed he couldn't understand why he had to remain behind to look after the farm. To him it was simple. A neighbour will run over and do it each day. He for sure had never lived on a farm.

When he walked away, I felt a sigh of relief. Maybe this will be his last visit, but that was not to be. Then he began to ask the children questions. I could not let that happen. They had done nothing to be put in this uncomfortable situation. As much as I did not wish to give him any reason to remove us from the train in some unknown lonely station, I told them to go for a slow walk so I could speak to the conductor.

The smirk on his face told me he thought I was now going to tell him all. Wrong. I told him, as politely as I could, that what I was doing was of no concern to him or anyone else. I did not appre-

ciate his questioning my children in front of me
or behind me. I have not and will not be breaking
any laws. Now please leave us alone. Should I have
need of your services, I will ask. Thank you. With
that I turned to the window leaving him no choice
but to move on.

Eventually darkness fell. There was nothing to
see but the dark passing by our window as though
it too was in a hurry to have morning come. We all
settled down for a snooze helping the time to pass.

I woke to the feel of the train slowing down.
The change in the movement told me we were nearing the station. It was time to prepare to leave.

After taking a couple days to get settled with
Martha and Dieter, I walked to the nearby elementary school to enrol Fritz and Katrin. This was the
first they had heard that they would not be in the
same class room. It had not occurred to me to prepare them for that. This was the biggest change
that they did not like. The teacher assured me that
the students would welcome them as they were all
friendly and willing to accept. That is not how Katrin saw it. I was afraid that the young girls would
notice that she was not dressed as well as they
were. I prayed they would be kind to her.

After a couple more days I went to Vancouver
with Martha's son to follow up on a lead she had
of a rooming house that had a vacant furnished
suite. The rooming house was across the street
from a park where I thought there would be others for them to play with. The park was a large
open square of lush green grass. They would need

to bring their own outdoor equipment. They had none, not even a ball. The elementary school was about four blocks away. They could walk. That would be just fine as that was the only way they knew of to get to school. Next I walked a couple blocks to a small business area to seek employment. There was a bakery that was ever so small but humming with activity. They were hiring. Now with a place to live and a job, we could move and begin to make a better life little by little, one of our own. It seems my life in the city is starting off just right.

A couple days later Martha and Dieter moved us and our three suitcases into the rooming house. The couple that owned it explained, once again, that they were making an exception to rent to me with children. They would need to be quiet and not disturb the others. We would need to share the bathroom with the other four tenants. I must have looked like I needed a helping hand. From that day on Mrs. Smith did her utmost to be of help. I am not so sure that Mr. Smith was as friendly to the idea of young ones in the home, but he was willing to give us a chance. The one that we needed.

Our suite was really a bachelor suite. There was a white four burner electric range that was clean but sported a few scratches and chips. It worked as did the oven. The cupboard had a four place setting of dishes with dainty flowers in pink, some pots and a cast iron frying pan. In the drawer I found cutlery for four, two plaid tea towels and a couple flowery hand towels along with a plain yellow pot holder. There was a second hand store within walking distance that I was sure would have anything else I might need. But first I needed a pay cheque.

The small drop leaf table in blue had three chairs sitting around it. They too were painted a matching blue.

Mrs. Smith had told me they had a cot they would set up against the wall for Fritz. I could have cried when I walked in and saw it covered with the necessary bedding including a pillow. Fritz loved his bed immediately, rushing over to sit on it.

The sitting room had a pull out couch that Katrin and I would share. It was not very comfortable but I was grateful that we had a bed to sleep on. There was a sitting chair in a rust and yellow coloured plaid pattern that sat in the corner. This was now home. Oh yes, in the other empty corner stood a Wardrobe Cabinet. It too was painted blue, just like the table and chairs. I didn't mind. I thought it looked clean and fresh. It had more room than we had clothes.

Our favourite part of our suite was where we stepped out onto a balcony from the sitting room. We all oohed and aahed over it. It was only big enough for four people, providing they were not very big, to stand at one time but we enjoyed it so much. Katrin said it made her feel as though she was on top of the world. There was seldom a day that we didn't go out there, if but for a few minutes to enjoy the yard below.

On our first day there, I took Katrin and Fritz for a walk to the school. Once there I went in search of the principal. After introducing my-self, I explained that we had just moved here from Saskatchewan. Then I explained about their edu-cation. I knew they were already behind as there were subjects that they never studied due to un-availability. Immediately I could tell that he did not understand this. He had no knowledge of real country living in the North. He seemed more in-terested in why I would be living in the city with-out a husband, and how I was planning to support them rather than their studies. With his manner of questioning I knew he was trying to make it clear to me that he did not approve. I did not like him speaking of things that I thought should not be spoken of in front of my children for fear of upset-ting them. I will need to make an appointment so I can set him straight in private. He is getting much too personal with my affairs.

I explained how I already had a job which seemed as though he couldn't think how that could be possible, after all I was a woman. After nu-merous questions, most of which I felt he didn't need to know let alone ask, he said their teachers would be expecting them in the morning. Before we turned to leave he called to each of them to re-member their room number. They would need that to find their way. There would be no one to assist them.

I was now beginning to find out how difficult life in the city could be. We would all need to learn to be strong and independent. Fritz would be fine, but I wasn't so sure Katrin would catch on as easily due to being so shy. I expected there to be days that each of us would feel as though we were not too steady on our feet, but we will stand firm and tall. We will make it.

I knew when we left Katrin was a little upset all the while trying to be brave. I now planned to take them for a walk to see where I would be working. My thought was that this would give their spirits a lift when they saw all the cookies. As we walked along I heard Fritz quietly say to Katrin that the Principal is a dunderhead. Normally I would not have ignored the remark, but I couldn't help but agree so I said nothing.

We walked back to the rooming house stopping for a few minutes to talk about the park. There was nothing more there than a large open field of green grass that appeared to be a little unhappy from the winter weather. I wished I could afford a ball for them to kick around, but that would have to wait. Then we left for the bakery.

Quality Bakery was located in the busy business area of Kingsway and Fraser Streets. This meant they would need a little bit more of a reminder of the traffic and lights. It seemed to me that there were vehicles going everywhere in every direction stopping for no one but a red light.

After having introduced them to the people I would be working with, they were each given a sugar cookie for the walk home. After lunch we would do both walks again, this time letting them lead the way. They had no trouble.

Soon Tuesday morning came. I needed to leave

for work at six. They had no need to get up until seven. Mrs. Smith said she would wake them. I was confident they would follow the instructions I had given them for the coming day. They were both excited to come home, by themselves, for lunch each day. I had promised them Wonder Bread with margarine. Tonight I would need to show them how to colour the margarine with the packet of bright yellow colouring that was included to make it look like real butter. They were fascinated with the colourful wrapping, having never seen bread packaged before. Being a typical mother I knew how bright they were, but also carried the fears of this new life they were unaccustomed to. Again I prayed they would be kept safe.

Following my instructions, Fritz and Katrin were to meet outside the main school door to walk home together. One particular day Katrin went out the wrong door. I must admit that each door was the same, all three of them. After waiting for a while with no brother coming, she decided to go home by herself. Having no sense of direction since we moved to the city, she turned the wrong way going to another area where the houses did not look familiar, and there was no park.

After wandering around for a while not seeing the now familiar park, she said she went to a door to ask for help to find her way. A lady with an abrupt manner answered the door. With tears in her eyes Katrin said that she was lost, and could she help her. The lady gruffly told her that was a lie, she knew her kind. She was there to steal her things. The lady then yelled at her telling her to leave now as she banged the door shut in her face. This now frightened Katrin more than ever.

With tears dripping down her cheeks, she said she then ran down the steps not stopping until she came to the end of the block and there and behold to her right she could see the park. Running the rest of the way home as fast as she could, she found her brother in the kitchen calmly eating his lunch.

Nothing was said to me about this adventure until a week later when I overheard them talking. Together they solved the problem. They had arranged a new meeting place inside the school. I was so proud of them. They would have to stick together, and continue to look after each other. Now I knew they would do so with more compassion for the other.

It was but a few weeks later that I discovered Dad's Bakery had a take-out window just down the street from Quality Bakery. By now I was baking bread instead of decorating cakes. The other baker, a nice man in his sixties with greying hair and a soft spoken voice, told me how they sell a brown lunch bag full of cookies for $0.25 each. You do not get to choose your favourite flavour, he explained. That was fine for me. I knew we would love them all. This was something we could afford.

So from then on, when I left for work on Saturday mornings I would leave a cookie quarter on the counter. At eleven o'clock in the morning they would eagerly walk over to the cookie window, as they called it. The kind lady would fill the bag as full as she could as well as giving them each one for the walk home. Somehow by the time I came home from work the bag was not brimming full. These were cookies that were not in perfect shape to sell in their boxes that went to the stores. However, they still had that delicious taste. The most important part.

Chapter Three

After we had been living in our cozy warm suite for a while, Fritz and Katrin informed me that Mrs. Smith's son was home for a while. His room was downstairs in the basement beside the washing machine room. He sits on the basement steps, plays his guitar and sings I was told. I had not heard anything about him, but they said he was the greatest singer ever.

"What is his name?" I asked.

"He said his name is Galen. They call him Hotfoot Smitty when he sings."

"So why don't they just call him Galen like his folks do?"

"Well, you see it is like this," he said to us. "I go places where I can play my guitar and sing for people. Then they pay me money. That is my job. You are supposed to use a different name when you are working."

They then proceeded to tell me how he doesn't have a horse. He has never even ridden one said Fritz as though he couldn't believe it.

"So what does he look like?" I asked.

Fritz then went into detail about his great looking black cowboy hat with a grey feather on one side. His cowboy boots were a shiny black with a black pattern on them. "That's all I saw," he said.

"Didn't he wear a shirt?" I asked.

As Fritz shrugged his shoulders and shook his head, Katrin said "Yes. It was blue squares, white squares and blue lines just like the ones Uncle Otto wore," she said.

I knew now that it was plaid, a bright blue plaid. "He must have had a guitar," I stated. Now Fritz's eyes lit up with excitement and wonder. I knew he was thinking of the guitar we had on the farm that was left behind. It was more of a play one that had been given to us by Mr. Sturge when he was ever so small. "It was a light brown with dark brown sides and back. "The strings were white," Fritz said as he pretended he was strumming his own guitar.

"Does slim mean skinny?" asked Katrin.

"Yes. That is the polite word. Now don't you two be in his way when he is practicing. If Galen doesn't mind you can listen, but you must not disturb him."

"He is old," stated Katrin.

Now it is time to let that pass. I guess when I am speaking to Mrs. Smith I shall ask her about her son so I can be prepared for further discussions. I am sure they will come.

I had still not made any new friends. My days were taken with work. I had Saturday afternoons and Sundays off. Sunday mornings we went to church.

The afternoons we walked around taking in the area as far as our feet would take us. There was a nice corner store, as Mrs. Smith called it. We just took a quick glance inside, but with not having extra money for treats I did not encourage them to look around. There were too many treats even for me to resist. It looked like a child's paradise. Every inch was covered with something that looked as though someone in your family would want even if they didn't need it. Once again I explained how we did not have money for unnecessary things. This seemed to be the one thing they have heard all their lives. I hope I can change that so that at least once in a while I can say for us to choose a treat.

The people at my work were friendly, but kept to themselves just as I did. Since Harold prepared the bread dough, some for loaves and others for buns, we worked close together with little time for conversation. We made cinnamon buns for the morning and dinner buns for lunch and supper. Each day we pulled pan after pan from the hot oven only to see them disappear before our eyes. There never seemed to be any left over at the end of the day only the delicious smell of cinnamon lingering in the air. Harold and I soon came to be known as the two best bread bakers around leaving us with a feeling of great pride. At the end of the day we returned home exhausted with aching arms and no leftover buns for us.

Lois was so busy baking cakes of all sizes that she too had no time or desire to say more than good morning as she entered hanging her brown jacket beside the door. When the day was over, her apron was hung by the back door that she promptly went through just as quickly taking her jacket with her. She too seemed to have no desire to speak to anyone, but she made beautiful cakes that were high in demand. Anytime I looked at her I had to smile. She was a tall lady of medium build with a striking appearance. She dressed very simply, but looked so fashionable. I am sure when she dressed for a night on the town she turned heads.

Thelma had become the new cake decorator and was doing a good job. She was a middle aged plump lady with long greying hair that she kept braided in a Dutch crown wrapped around the back of her head. She spoke no English, only Norwegian. When she arrived in the mornings, she gave anyone that cared to notice a smile that showed her glistening white teeth. One that had to do for the whole day.

The only other person there was Nola. She was a kind no nonsense lady with no time for extra words. Sometimes when a customer commented on the weather, her quick look told them she had no time for idle chatter, but they still liked her. Each day she baked a few pans of sugar cookies. With Dad's Cookie Company just doors away we did not have much demand for cookies. Nola looked after all the customers smiling to them and each of us throughout the day as she passed us by without sharing any words. What else she did I did not know, nor was it any of my concern.

Since Harold had been working there the longest as well as being a little older, he knew how to get on the good side of Nola. Soon he had it arranged that we could take our lunch break at the same time. Now this took some careful planning on our part. There was a chair in the closet that contained brooms and mops that I was able to sit on at his insistence. He turned a pail upside down for himself. This was the lunch room. Soon he began to remind me of my dear friend Mr. Bosch. I missed him so much. Almost as much as Floyd.

Besides Floyd, Harold was the only man I had seen wearing overalls each and every day. Actually Floyd always wore his suit, shirt and tie for church. Harold's shirt was a light brown colour. Each day the same. The grey in his hair left only enough of a reddish colour to let you know where the brown spots on his nose came from. His round face was always brimming with kindness.

One day as I walked home from work I realized that little by little Harold had found a soft way to get me to share my feelings with him by himself opening up to me, or maybe he too needed someone to talk to.

He told me how his wife that he had loved so much had passed away ten years ago. No one really knew what it was, he had said. She had been having terrible pains in her tummy to which there seemed to be no relief. When she no longer could eat she began to shrink away. By that time she was shrinking into herself. It was as though she was in her own world, one that he could not reach. One day the doctor said there was nothing they could do. Keep her at home where she is warm and comfortable, he was told. When he went to work the neighbour would look in on her. She was his life. Some days he seems so despondent, others he is the happy man we know.

Harold only had one son that had left home for somewhere in parts unknown. He had left in search of work with promises to return in one year. It has now been twelve years with no word. He would not even know that his Momma has passed. Harold said he no longer worries about that, but I knew that deep down he does. What seems to bother him the most is wondering if he is alive and in good health. I could not help but wonder if he looked like his daddy or his momma, not that it matters one iota.

Since he has not shared these thoughts and feelings with anyone else, I would not dream of doing so either. That is for him to tell, and him alone.

So far I have not revealed too much of my life. It still hurts way too much. It is never far from my mind. Many nights I spend tossing and turning. It will take me a long time to be convinced that I made the correct decision. Already when I see the progress Fritz and Katrin have made with their studies I know it was one I had to make. Not the easy one.

They both seem so ambitious. Katrin has asked the neighbour lady if she could baby-sit for her. Between this lady and another, she seems to be baby-sitting at least two times a week. The responsibility is good for her. While she receives ten cents an hour it does not give her much money to spend, but it is a little.

Fritz has now got a paper route delivering close to one hundred news papers six days a week with an old pull cart given to him by the previous paper carrier. He loves his spending money, and spend it he does. There are times when he finds it difficult to collect from some of his customers so I then need to go with him on his next attempt. He usually is successful at collecting it then. This seems to be a mean lesson for a youngster to have to learn but seems it is part of city life.

As spring is now arriving with some mild evenings for us to enjoy, I try to spend a little while in the evening sitting on the front steps watching the city life happen. Each day the trees seemed to sprout new leaves to cover their bare branches as the weather warms. Nancy Tutton, another lady from the rooming house, began to stop and visit with me. I found her to be friendly but not nosey. Soon we became good friends. As she worked down town she had little time for social life. There was always one extra hour added on to each end of her day for travelling.

Several months later the leaves on the trees were showing off their fresh rich colours leaving each tree looking full and bushy. They were telling us that spring was here. The days were milder with the sun shinning down like a warm blanket covering us. The evenings were still brisk leaving only a short time to relax on the front porch.

One particular evening as I was reaching the top of the stairs to go to our room, I heard a soft voice, "Emma, Emma, do you have a minute to talk?"

"Yes, I do. What is it Nancy?"

"It is supposed to be sunny out on Sunday. I was wondering if we both hurried home from church if we could take Fritz and Katrin to Stanley Park for a while. I have a picnic basket that we could take a lunch with us. We will not have too far to walk after we get off the bus."

"Sounds like a good idea. I have been waiting for the day when we could go there. We will hurry home for sure."

"We will not be able to see very much of it in one trip but it is a start. The beautiful swans will be slowly swimming by in the clear waters of Lost Lagoon as we begin our walk. If I don't get to see you before I will see you then."

"Yes, for sure. Good night Nancy."

"Good night Emma."

That night as I lay in bed I felt more excitement than I had felt for a long time. It was a feeling of a happy stress free day. One that I felt I needed to lighten my burden. I must not accidentally tell Fritz and Katrin. Perhaps on Saturday when I get home from work will be a good time for that.

The next morning as I walked to work thinking of lunch break with Harold, I would tell him of my Sunday plans. Already I could hear him telling me how happy he was for me. I felt as though I was skipping as I walked.

It was shortly before our lunch break that I really noticed the strain on Harold's face. I had been too wrapped up in my own world to notice my friend. I suddenly felt ashamed. It only took a moment for me to see the pain on my friend's face. Something was terribly wrong. The best I could do at the moment was to give him a quick pat on the shoulder sending him a private message that I knew he was hurting. Giving me a slight nod he turned back to the mound of dough laying before him, but not without my seeing the water build in his light brown eyes.

From that moment on I found myself going through the motions of kneading dough, rolling dough and shaping dough. It was like I was just a machine on automatic giving no thought to what I was doing.

As soon as we were seated in our tiny lunch room, I looked at my friend to see that he was near breaking. For sure his heart was hurting.

"Oh Harold. What is the trouble?"

In a breaking voice, he said, "It is my son Huey. Someone dropped him off late last night at my door. When I heard a loud thump I looked out to see if it was just kids playing. There I saw a crumpled dishevelled man laying in a heap at the top of the stairs. Somehow I knew it was Huey."

As he sat with his head in his hands, elbows resting on his knees, I knew he just could not talk. We sat there for a while not saying anything, me with my arm around his shoulders, Harold trying to control his tears. When I felt him pat my hand with his, I knew that he was now in control once again.

"I am so sorry Harold. Our hearts always break for our children no matter how old they are. Do not feel ashamed. You are just showing the compassion and love in your heart for your son. I am proud to have you for my friend."

As I was speaking, Nola poked her head in as though she was about to say something. After a short moment, she said, "Hey you two, take an extra ten. We have everything under control."

Before returning myself to Harold, I quickly mouthed 'Thank you' to Nola. With a silent nod she turned and left.

I just sat there not sure as to what he needed to hear. Then Harold turned to me. "You are a good friend. Just what I needed today. I am not sure what I shall do with his sorry state but I now feel I can deal with it. He looks as if he has been living in the back alleys of Victory Square. My own son, too proud to return home. Now I have another problem. The rooming house I live in will not allow us to have overnight guests never mind permanent. I will be given a week to move even if he is to move out today. I broke the landlord's rules by keeping my son last night. What was I to do?"

As much as it broke my heart I knew that I had to return to work. It would not help for me to loose my job. Perhaps I can whisper a few words to Nola for her help.

As though she read my mind, as soon as I returned to my table she whispered, "Is it Huey?"

I just nodded a yes to her. How could she have known, I wondered. Is this a repeat problem? Then she turned and headed to our little lunch room. I wanted to pray for Harold but I couldn't think of what to ask for first.

From the corner of my eye I saw my friend leave by the back door. As Nola walked up to me, she quietly said, "Please remain behind for a couple minutes at the end of the day."

If ever I wished I had some dough to knead, it was now. It can relieve so much tension. It seemed like the end of our shift would never come, but come it did. I felt grateful that I did not have to leave with Harold's burden on my shoulders. There must be a way to help my friend.

It turns out that Nola and her husband know his landlords. While the landlady has a heavy hand, which is perhaps needed, her husband has a soft heart underneath her hand. They will not evict them, she said she felt sure of that.

She then told of how her husband Frank worked for a large warehouse. He will speak to his boss in the morning. I know he will. Perhaps Huey will get a job there sweeping floors, but first he will need to seek help to clean his life up. They will not tolerate an employee arriving at work in the morning with the smell of leftover alcohol on his breath. Not even moonshine. Help will be there for him, but he will need to commit to do his part or he will be let go. He will not be given any warnings.

The next few days we were so busy filling the extra orders for buns, both plain and cinnamon, that Harold and I were not able to take our break at the same time. I did notice that his spirits seemed a little better as the days moved on. For him I thought it was a good thing for the sudden burst of orders. By the time we went home at the end of our shift, I am sure he too was too tired to lay awake all night with worry.

A few days later Nola whispered to me that

Frank had said that Huey was trying to stay clean. Some of his street buddies had shown up outside waiting for him to finish his shift. While Frank detained Huey, his boss put the run on them in no uncertain terms. Stay away or we will call the police, they were told. They each knew they had too much against them to take a chance, for sure charges would be laid. They would be spending more than one night in jail. They knew that the police knew who was drinking moonshine. It was just as illegal to buy it as to sell it.

It seemed that while Huey did not know it, he had a wall of guardian angels around him trying their best to protect him.

Sunday morning I woke to what appeared to have the makings of a perfect day. The sky was a beautiful blue with a covering here and there of white hairnets. The trees barely swayed with the passing wispy white clouds overhead.

As we hurried home from church walking as quickly as we could so as to have some time for a little lunch before leaving for the bus, Fritz and Katrin asked many questions as to what there would be to see. I took this opportunity to tell them what Harold had told me of the history of Stanley Park.

"It was named after Lord Stanley, a British politician. It was Vancouver's first public park covering one thousand acres." Neither myself or my children could even begin to imagine just how big that is.

"Besides the animals, there are many things to see that are unique to the park."

"Like what ?" asked Katrin. "Pink ice cream?"

"Well, there is a giant hollow tree. We can all stand in the hollow at once. At least that is what Harold told me yesterday."

"So, can we climb it?" asked Fritz.

"No. There are many trees in the park, but no one is allowed to climb them. Just like no one is allowed to pick the flowers. They are there for all to see and enjoy, not just us. The flowers are just like the flowers on the farm in the field. If we pick them there will not be any to seed for next year."

While neither one said anything regarding the past, I was relieved to see the rooming house just ahead. As they both took off running, I said no running in the house to no one but me. They were too far ahead to hear.

Just as we reached the bottom of the stairs, Mrs. Smith came in through the front door.

"So where are you all going that brings so much excitement?"

"We are going on a bus," said Katrin.

"Then we are going to Stanley Park," said Fritz with a smile that went from one side of his face to the other.

"Well, have fun and don't forget to read the Buzzer on the bus. Bye," and with that she was going inside her suite gently closing the door behind her.

Last night before getting ready for bed we talked about bus manners. I explained to them they would sit together, but if anyone older got on and there was not enough empty seats they were to get up giving their seats to someone else. They both said they would but not with too much enthusiasm.

It didn't seem to take too long until I could see Lost Lagoon ahead surrounded by a rich evergreen forest of lush plant life like a giant horseshoe. A high water fountain in the middle sprayed water pummelling down into the bottom leaving a spray behind to glisten in the sunlight. This must be the exquisite Jubilee Fountain that Harold spoke of. Just like he said it is gracing the North East end of Lost Lagoon. He said it was installed in 1936 as a Centennial Gift to the City of Vancouver where 600 people were living at that time. We were aah struck. We must come back, if not just to see this beautiful fountain closer to Christmas when it is lit up in reds and greens to resemble a Christmas tree. Almost more than I could imagine.

There was so much to see in this big city as the bus rolled along I couldn't take it all in, not to mention Gastown with it's big Steam clock. Fritz would like to see the giant Statue of Gassy Jack, also in Gastown. This bus will be carrying us along for many a fun trip to come.

As we got closer I could see the white swans swimming aimlessly about. As we left the bus to walk closer to the lake, a pair of light grey swans emerged from the grasses as they waddled towards their friends. What a beautiful serene sight it was. Swans are closely related to geese and ducks, I told them. Swans have long necks and vary in colour from a snow white to greys, browns and coal black depending on their species. They certainly knew what coal looked like. While I did like the white swans the best, each was beautiful in its' own way. I was so glad that I was able to remember at least some of the things Harold had been telling me.

As we walked along the path going further into the park, there became more and more trees each rich in colour from light greens to dark greens and to red cedars. The grey squirrels scurrying back and forth from one tree to the other kept us amused for much too long as we watched them with their bushy tails carrying pine cones to their nests to enjoy for dinner later in the day.

Nancy and I thought it to be a good idea to walk over to where the children's zoo is. This would interest them while we sat on the grass to enjoy a bite to eat from her Wicker picnic basket and rest our weary feet. It was too early in the season for seasonal bushes to bloom, but we enjoyed their rich green leaves as we anticipated their beautiful blossoms to come.

Dear Nancy, she knew just what to bring. A true picnic lunch. There were fresh hotdog buns buttered with margarine and mustard for the cold wieners to be wrapped inside. Soft oatmeal cookies for our dessert to be washed down with sweetened lemonade securely sealed in jars with tight fitting lids to prevent any leaks.

While Nancy and I sat and watched my children run from one place to the other trying to see all the animals at once, we chatted letting our tired feet rest a little while longer as we did some people watching at the same time. They did remember to check to be sure they could still see me which meant I could see them, why I don't know. They would not get lost. Fritz had a great sense of direction. Katrin would be right beside him.

Nancy had assured them they would not be able to see all the animals in one day giving us a reason to return on another sunny day. We talked of how this was something I could afford to do on a Sunday afternoon. If we were careful we could save bus fare for a once a month trip to this beautiful park. Nancy assured me that if she could, she would be happy to come along.

As we walked back to board our bus for our ride home we heard the clip-clop of a horse's hoofs on the trail, made from old logging skids, from behind us. Knowing we had enough time, we stopped to see who was coming. Much to their surprise it was a policeman wearing his dark blue uniform with a matching blue and white helmet riding on a magnificent looking white horse. As we stopped to let him go by, he stopped to let them rub his nose. He told them that his name was Officer Martin. His partner was Chief. They had been working together for three years. They were best friends. Of course, he then asked them what their names were and what grade they were in. When I suggested that it was time for us to go to the bus stop, they said their good-bys as Officer Martin said he would be watching for them another day. Clicking his tongue, he urged Chief ahead to continue on their path checking out the park before leaving for the day.

Chapter Four

A few weeks later things had settled in to a more stable routine both at home and at work. I had made a few friends through the rooming house and church. We had been invited for Sunday dinner a few times to the home of a family from church. They were a large family with eight children ranging in age from ten up to eighteen. I thought of them as being very generous and giving people.

Their sixteen year old daughter Sarah drew my attention the most. She was perhaps a little taller than most girls her age, but with her long black hair and fair complexion she was a beauty. While they were all well mannered, friendly young people, there was something about Sarah. She was definitely her own person. The most outgoing of them all. Her parents tried to be firm with their house rules, but dear Sarah managed around them winning everyone over with her charming smile.

Going to church each Sunday morning was a must in their house. Each Saturday evening she went out with her group of friends promising to be home early to be sure she would be up in time for church. Just as she promised, Sarah was there in time for the service to start sometimes walking in with the Pastor.

As her mother said she had explained to all her children many times, when we go to church we are going to God's House so we wear our best. Well, Sarah thought she did. Perhaps not her best, but her favourite.

In the very early 1950's it was not proper for girls and ladies to go out wearing slacks instead of a dress as it was not considered lady like. But not Sarah. She said her favourites were her best, like her loose hanging black drape pants and a shirt style blouse in red. Most Sundays her hair was worn in big curlers with a kerchief tied over as she had not had time to comb it in order to not be late for service just like her dad had said. The congregation tried their best to pretend they had not noticed, but notice they did.

When service was over Sarah smiled as she said hello to everyone while she left the Chapel. Now who couldn't love that girl. I felt she had taken a little bit of a shine to me more so as she knew that I too had broken tradition receiving some criticism.

These were the years when it was almost unheard of for a woman to leave the home no matter what the condition or reason might be. Even those with a husband who was not kind or providing. There was no excuse. It was her job to make sure that ends were met as though she could pull a magic string and it would come. The farm wives were expected to work like a man as well as be the wife, mother, teacher, doctor etc. It was not considered necessary for a woman to get an education. Her job did not require it. If she was strong with endless energy, and had an ability to cook she would make a good wife.

I could not forget how hard I worked over the years, as did Floyd, only being able to survive. He was adamant that it was not necessary for Fritz to get further education as he would be a farmer. As for Katrin, she didn't need it either as I could teach her all she needed to know about cooking and sewing. She already knew more than most girls her age. All her dad wanted for her was to marry a farmer's son that lived close to us. I wanted more.

As I stood outside after service making light conversation with the other ladies, I could tell they were wondering about my life thinking things they felt better not to say. I did my best to make light conversation discussing general topics like the weather etc. Somehow whenever I felt there was someone nearing me that was for sure going to ask questions they didn't need to know, Sarah seemed to be at my side followed closely by her mother. How could I have possibly had two better friends I did not know.

After several invitations to their home for Sunday dinner I began to speak more openly with Hazel, Sarah's mother. She told me how her sister too is not having an easy life with no possibility of an education for any of her six children, and no education in sight. While I did not feel I could bare my soul, I know she was able to put together many unsaid things. Each time we parted she handed me a plate with fresh cake to take home or some other treat leaving me with an assurance that we were always welcome, she would have a listening shoulder. As kind as she was, I couldn't seem to share my burden.

One Monday as I was busy kneading bread dough at the bakery, my thoughts were deep in

memory of our delicious dinner the evening before, when I suddenly realized that Harold was
late for work. This was totally unheard of. He was
the most predictable employee they had ever had,
according to Nola. We were just like a family, each
concerned for the other. Just about the time I was
going to panic, the back door opened and in walked
Harold, eyes glued to the floor with sagging shoulders that said they were carrying the weight of the
world. Without a glance around he began preparing his usual batch of bread dough. As we all went
about our work it seemed as though it took forever
for break time to come. I sat on my pail expecting
him to come in at any time, but no one entered. I
waited until the last second for my friend to enter
before I returned to the inside of the bakery where
the air was so very hot from the large ovens dis-
pelling their heat each time the doors were opened.
It seemed to drain the energy from us. I certainly
had never before experienced so much heat in one
room. Even during the hot summer months when
I was baking bread in our little log house it wasn't
this hot. There the flies were visiting so much that
I had to have sticky yucky fly strips hanging to
catch them. How nice to not have flies in a kitchen.

Walking back to my little work table I noticed
the others were keeping their eyes on their tables
as though there wasn't another soul in the world.
Their faces had not a slight sign of a smile. Shoulders were slumped with a heavy weight they too
carried for Harold. With all the activity going on,
one could have heard a mouse running across the

rough plank wood floor. Only the bread dough squeaked as Harold kneaded his mound harder and harder.

It was but minutes before our lunch break that the back door burst open with two big burly men heading straight for Harold. Paying no attention to Nola speaking to them, they pushed their way between the fancy cakes and cinnamon buns. Lola was frantic. As she shouted for them to leave they ignored her until the one nearest to her seemed to have had enough. With one hand he threw her to the floor like a rag doll. It only took a moment before she was slowly bringing herself to her feet, cursing a blue streak. I felt as though I was frozen in place just like the clothes were when I brought them inside the little log house during the winter time. I would stand them on the floor to thaw before putting them away. It looked as though some colourful ghosts were visiting.

This was an area that no one without a large white apron to cover their clothing as well as wearing a hair net was permitted for sanitary reasons. I wondered if we would be breaking a health law. I did know that if they touched anything either baked or to be baked, it would need to be thrown away. Nola was so proud of the high standard this bakery had achieved. She was determined that Quality Bakery would always be just that, the finest quality.

With two more heavy steps they were beside Harold. Without a word they began to drag my friend by his arms to the back door. I had to help.

I could not just stand there. Feeling as though my body had been lifted through the air, I found myself standing in front of the door screaming at the top of my lungs that they had to let him go. It was then that I realized Harold had fainted at their hands, but they continued to drag his lifeless body toward the door.

Lois and Thelma then seized the moment to attack, and attack they did. They jumped on their backs pulling their hair screaming for all they were worth with one hand pushing their thumbs into the throats of the two mean thugs. Nola accidentally kicked over a couple pails that made a racket for all to hear. As the two thugs dressed in black suits and dark glasses began to fight back trying to rid themselves of two mean females, a man from a near business was taking items to the garbage bin. Hearing and seeing the commotion he too began to holler for help. Picking up a large stick he charged the men wielding his weapon as though it were a machete.

Suddenly I found myself being pushed over hitting my head against the wall as I fell to the floor. The kind neighbour had been hit over the back of his head and was now laying on the floor near me bleeding badly. They had a mean burly accomplice dressed in black that had been waiting for them. It seems that when they took too long he decided to investigate.

These three burly thugs were no match for us. Dropping Harold like a sack of potatoes, they decided to leave with a stiff warning to Harold that they would find him. I heard one say something that they would be back to collect the $200 his no good son owed him. We will not forget, they angrily shouted as they kicked him and spat on him before leaving.

Our first task was to be sure Harold was alright. While he was a little slow getting up, he was soon on his feet holding the side of his head assuring us he will be just fine. After checking each other over, we decided that the worst we may be left with will be a few bruises and a bad memory of this ordinary day. For Harold, it seems he will have much more to deal with.

Over the next few days as we ate our lunch Harold shared with me how Huey's past was coming back to visit him. It seems that shortly after he left home, he went into a bar, just to see what it was all about. While sitting at a table by himself nursing a beer, some other men came in. Without his invitation they sat at his table, just to keep him company for a while they told him through their loud unruly laughter. He tried to insist that he just wanted to have alone time which only seemed to hype them up more. While one was trying to outdo the other with his smart talk, the others were ordering more beers for them to share. They were saying things like you are our new friend, we will look after you, hang out with us and you will be safe.

After quickly drinking a few more beers, Huey said he knew he had to leave while he was still able to walk. Getting up from his chair he began to

sway from side to side. Since Huey was only accustomed to having an occasional beer it now had
its' effect on him. The biggest guy with bad breath
put his arm around his shoulders telling him how
they were now friends. He would not let anything
happen to him over and over again. Soon he found
himself not being able to hear everything that was
said to him. They were laughing so loud Huey said
he thought his head would burst from the noise.
He didn't know how long it was before he passed
out.

When he woke up it was morning. The light
of day was shinning down on him with only the
cold damp earth beneath him. His new friends
were gone. He was in a back alley somewhere. Just
where he did not know.

His billfold was laying on the ground near him.
Both his dollar bills were missing. He still carried
the few pennies and nickels he had had in his pants
pocket. He knew now that he was as good as broke
and didn't know where he was or where his new
friends were. He would need to locate the old shed
in someone's yard that he had been calling home.

Huey then walked around to find the front of
the buildings only to find that there was no bar,
nor was there one anywhere around that he could
see. He said he walked until he became so tired he
could no longer go on. Still he did not know where
he was. He could not see a sign of anything familiar. Not wishing to be found in an alley by himself,
he sat on the front steps of a old worn out looking
building that may house some offices. It was clean

but needed paint. What it did have was beginning to peel off giving an even older look to the once new building.

By now the sun had shone brightly bringing its' warmth to him, but now it too was leaving him behind and alone. His mind now started telling him that he just had to find his way before dark. But how? His stomach was telling him he was hungry, very hungry.

As he walked along he began to smell food. Just what kind he did not know, but he did know it would taste real good. As he was passing an alley, he saw a door open. A man wearing a large white apron stepped out as though to put something in the garbage can. Huey said as he walked towards him they both looked into each other's eyes. All Huey could see was warmth and compassion. Maybe he had found the help he needed.

As Huey neared, the other man asked if he was lost. Before Huey knew it he was pouring his story out to this kind stranger. Without a moments hesitation he was invited inside to the kitchen of a hamburger joint that just happened to have a couple left over hamburgers with buns. This stranger told him they had his name all over them so eat up. When I am finished cleaning I will help you find home. Huey knew that he had tears in his eyes from such generosity.

You know Emma, my Huey remembered his upbringing he told me. He picked up the broom sweeping the floor for this kind stranger that had just fed him.

He walked me to where he lived, about a block away, in a small older home of wood and stone. It appeared to have been some time since this friendly looking home had been painted a pretty brown the colour of hot steaming coffee. Huey said when they reached the back yard of neatly mowed green grass surrounded by a picket fence that at one time was white, he was told to wait there. He would be right back. Now he began to wonder if yet again he had walked into a trap. One that would once again swallow him up leaving him to die on the barren dirt ground by himself.

Just as he was going to leave before the worst could happen to him again, this stranger came out of his house with his hand stretch out to Huey.

"My name is Gaston. Gaston Hatcher. What is your name?" the stranger asked.

"Huey. Huey Razner. My Pa is Harold Razner," he said he told him.

"Well, I have an offer for you. Since you do not have work, how would you like to work for me at the hamburger joint? I call it The Mrs. Funny name don't you think? Everyone thinks my Mrs. does the cooking but she is too busy with our five youngsters to help out. You could live in this shed that my brother had lived in before he went away. You see, he left one morning and never came back. He was supposed to be helping me at The Mrs I would do the cooking while you would do the cleaning. Would that work for you? We can travel back and forth together." but guess he didn't like it much. We could work together if you would like.

With that Huey said he couldn't say no. He would have a place to stay that was warm and a job to go to. He said the pay was not the highest but he felt it was fair for the work he did. As long as he was satisfied with a hamburger and some fries, lunch was free. They gave him some oatmeal that he could cook for his breakfasts, some wieners and beans for a few suppers, and a pot of stew with a loaf of bread. By then it would be pay day. He would be on his own. I would say that this Gaston is a very generous man.

Huey said he soon fell into a routine working six days a week. Rather than spend the extra day at home by himself, he chose to work enjoying the company of the customers as he cleared the tables. He came to know many of them by name. Everyone knew his name he proudly said. They looked forward to seeing him especially a young lady named Hazel.

It took a little persuasion on my part, but little by little he began to share with me of his friend Hazel. Sometimes he had that dreamy look on his face that showed he had fallen in love. But then the next moment when he spoke of her his eyes would well up and get all watery.

Over a period of time he has come to tell me of Hazel. As I guessed he was real smitten with her from the beginning and she with him. Actually I think he liked her a lot. He kept saying how they were just really good friends. They told each other all kinds of things that they never shared with anyone else. That is what friends do, I guess. Just like us.

"So what happened?" I asked him.

"She died," was Huey's flat reply to me said Harold.

Harold then told me how he was so shocked he did not know what to say for a couple moments. After sharing with his son how important it is to have a good friend that one can share their worries with, he expressed how sorry he was to hear of such a tragic thing. Hazel was nineteen just like Huey. Apparently Hazel was just like Huey in that she too was just trying to find the right job that would be hers for many years to come. All Huey knew was that she had been having some awful headaches for a while, but had not seen a doctor. Unfortunately, another young person that could not afford the medical care needed. Harold thinks it was this time that Huey was not feeling too well thereby being very vulnerable to anyone wishing to take advantage of a quiet lonely young man.

"So, how long has Huey been home?" I asked.

"He arrived back just after I came home from work on Friday. We spent some time just being happy to see each other. Just looking at my boy I knew he had something to tell. When he became quiet I knew he was ready."

"We sat up late into the night talking. I was so surprised to learn that he had been living in Penticton, which is not very far away. It is a pretty town in the Okanagan Valley between Okanagan and Skaha Lakes. You should go there some day. You will like it," he said.

He told me how Gaston thought it was a good idea for him to go home for the weekend. He could manage for one day alone. So as soon as he cleaned up after his lunch break, he took his back pack and set out on the Highway 3 with his thumb out asking drivers to give him a ride. The third car stopped for him.

It was an older couple, both with white hair and friendly smiles. Their old Studebaker in a fawn brown with vinyl interior, was clean and inviting. They told me they were Mr. & Mrs. Brown, just like their car, laughing at their own joke. By now I had learned that everyone that didn't want to tell you their real name said it was Brown. I couldn't help but smile as I said my name was Huey. With that Mr. Brown said uh huh, sure. I just let it go at that knowing full well he didn't believe me.

After sharing the usual pleasantries, Mrs. Brown said she hoped I was hungry because they like to munch as they drive. All I could think of to say was that is nice. I didn't think I should say good, because I am hungry. Two seconds later my stomach let out a loud growl that sent them both into fits of laughter, and my face a beet red hot as a fire in the cook stove.

It was so good to hear his voice being comfortable with his story that I couldn't stop smiling. I just waited for him to continue.

In a shake of a lamb's tail she said for me, I guessed I was Sonny, to open the box on the seat beside me. Out came the most delicious waft of salami sandwiches of thick white bread that had been buttered and spread with mustard just the way I had dreamed of them. Then I was told to open that jar beside the sandwiches. I reached back into the box to find a large jar filled with big green dill pickles that smelled rich in garlic, enough to make one take a second smell. I thought how this car shall not smell the same again. This was garlic heaven. In the box was also a jar with water in it that was obvious we were going to share straight from the jar. If they didn't mind, I wasn't going to mind. After the jar of clear water had been passed around, Sonny was told to take out the brown bag. Inside were the best tasting big, and I mean big, oatmeal with raisin cookies I had ever eaten. I think there was cinnamon in them too. They were so delicious, just like the rest of the munchies. I was assured that in a while we will have some more.

When we arrived in Vancouver Mrs. Brown insisted they drive me to my Pa's house. Mr. Brown did as it was firmly suggested he do. I thanked them ever so much for their kindness. They kept telling me how happy they were to help, it made me feel so humble and grateful. As I got out of the car, Mr. Brown called, "Oh Sonny, maybe one day you can do the same for someone else." With a wave, they were off.

Chapter Five

The months had flown by. Fritz had settled into the new school and new friends easily. While Katrin was now making her way too, it did not come as easy. Instead of there being fifteen to twenty students in the school, there were more than that in each class. For Katrin this was over whelming. Some grades had more than one class. We were now living in a large city where not all people were accepted as equal like in the small town area in the North.

This was not long after the World War 11 had ended. There were still many people that did not put it behind them. We were German and that was in no way a popular thing to be. On the farm no one cared, but I was certain that was not the way of the city. Many people believed that due to the disaster in the War, all German people were bad, and condoned the ideals of Hitler. Not so. I stressed many times over that they were not to say anything about us being German. They were to say that they did not know anything about it. If asked if we spoke German they were to say no. That was basically the truth, we did not speak it. I changed the pronunciation of our surname. To my knowledge no one asked. With my working hours I had not made any new friends in our neighbourhood. Katrin was babysitting next door some Saturday evenings, so I met them. They seemed like a nice family, but other than to say hello should I see them on the weekend there was no more communication.

One evening after dinner dishes of wieners, baked beans and mashed potatoes were cleared away, Katrin said she had something to ask about her teacher. Not having the slightest idea, I calmly said, "What is it?"

She explained how there was a boy and a girl, in the class that were Jews. She thought they were cousins. Their teacher was a German man. He talked to the class how only the Germans were good people, and the Jews were the scum of the earth. Before the class went outside at lunch time and recess time, he told them they were not to talk to or play with them because they were dirty Jews. Each day when they came back into the class room their desks were covered with stuff from the garbage cans. He had the class laugh at them while he said nasty stuff about them. She said it wasn't funny, they were both nice. She also told me how whenever papers needed to be handed in, the teacher always put two big red lines through their work going from one corner to the other touching in the middle. Suddenly I felt sick. My best friend Mary had been a Jew.

I knew they had never gone to church as there was no synagogue within travelling distance. That did not mean that they did not keep their beliefs and way of worshiping within their home. However was I going to get Katrin to accept something I have never condoned.

The best I could think of at that moment was to explain that she should not get involved, continue to be nice to both of them, do not take part in belittling anyone all the while trying not to get that teacher to be upset with her. I needed time to talk to my friend Harold.

That night as I lay in bed with eyes wide open, I thought of how the principal was so opposed to my life. He made it clear to me that my place was on the farm doing whatever my husband had said. Not once had he ever mentioned anything about my children's welfare. Clearly he did not care. I did. I was determined they would have a better chance at life. A mother will give up her soul for her children. Every night I worried that he would report me should my husband be looking for me. I knew he would try his best to take my children back to the farm.

I did not dare to ruffle any feathers. I knew Katrin was not happy with my decision to not help her friends. She did not know what was at stake for us. I would not explain that to my children.

Over the next few lunch breaks I told Harold about my situation as well as of the school principal. He agreed with me that it was not right, but very likely no one wanted to get on his wrong side. We both felt strong that other teachers had to be aware of the happenings in his class, but were not willing to get themselves into any difficult situations they would not be able to handle. Above all, he urged me not to go to either the teacher or the principal. To ruffle the principals' feathers would be sure to make life more difficult than we could handle. This was life in the city.

I felt the best I could do for them was to assure them that if they were nice to their classmates not taking part in saying anything that was not nice, they would be fine. Next year Katrin would have a different teacher that Fritz said was really nice, at least so his friends all said. None of his friends had liked Katrin's teacher either.

Nancy continued to go with us on our occasional visits to Stanley Park. I was now able to contribute more to the picnic basket. After a while Jack, another tenant in the rooming house, began to join us. He did not contribute to the picnic basket, but treated us all to an ice cream cone before heading to the bus that would take us home. Of course, pink for Katrin.

Soon Christmas was upon us. Our apartment was too small for a tree, but I did manage to purchase them each a small present. We would be going to Martha's house for Christmas. I still could not afford very much that was special for treats, but I did manage to make it a little nicer for them. Maybe next year I can do better.

One Saturday when I finished work at noon, I hurried home to change my clothes. Just as Nancy promised, she would take us on the bus to downtown Vancouver to see the decorations in Woodward's Department store. Fritz and Katrin were ready to go, bouncing with the excitement of this new life in the city. As much as she had tried to describe it to us, we were not able to picture such a fairy tale sight. I could not imagine that it would be prettier than anything we had seen while staying with Ursula.

Just as promised, we passed by huge trees standing outside on the green grass decorated with lights, topped with a big sparkly silver star on the top. A glittery thick rope was loosely wrapped around from the top to the bottom holding each in a gentle hug. Some trees had a rope of gold, some silver, some in red while others were white. The lights were an array of colours that were sure to glow in the dark of the night. Perhaps it will be dark by the time we return so we can enjoy their beauty at its' fullest.

We passed a homey looking house with the front steps lined with deep green boughs accented with large red bows on the hand rails. At the top was a large sign that said Merry Christmas in bright red letters. It looked so inviting that I could have skipped all the way to the top just to see who was home. One day my home will look just like that.

Once we were inside the store, the first department we walked through was the China Department. There were tables set in pretty red and green. Tables of wood with round red placemats topped with white plates holding a red poinsettia made of quilted fabric with a sparkly silver centre. Red and white serviettes in fan shapes were held up in tall cut glass wine goblets. Green boughs of fresh cut cedar with pine cones decorated the table. Beside each place mat lay a set of shiny silver flatware. Only the guests were missing.

As we were about to enter an area that displayed cookie jars of every description they spied a large gingerbread house all decorated with icing in white. There were red and white striped candy canes made of icing marking the edge of the walls. Above the door were hearts made of red and white ropes of sweet sugary icing. A gingerbread man and his wife stood beside the door waiting for it to open. The roof of snowy white icing was coated with jelly beans in an array of yummy colours.

As we strolled through the store going from one department to the other, Santa's helpers could often be found talking to the children that were eager to tell of all the things they hoped Santa would bring. Whenever Fritz and Katrin were stopped they did not know how to answer. I quickly added just a little surprise would be nice for them to which Santa's helper agreed. Leaving them with an assurance that he would be sure to tell Santa how good they had been all year, I just know you have. With a smile and a wink he was off to greet other children. If only he knew what they had been through. It was best that as few as possible knew our story.

Small trees stood on tables amongst the merchandise showing off the many tree ornaments there were just waiting to be taken home for a shoppers' tree to be enjoyed by their families. Holly with rich red berries and fresh green leaves were placed amidst the smaller items. Bows of a bright red plastic ribbon decorated the purses and handkerchiefs for ladies.

In the children's wear were mannequins the size of ten year olds wearing the latest in fashion for both boys and girls. I am sure I felt worse than they did especially seeing the little patent shoes for young girls. My poor Katrin was sill wearing second hand brown oxford shoes with well worn toes from too many scuff marks. Oh dear. I must think of finding a job that pays more.

Before leaving for home I promised them they could take a couple more rides up to the top floor and down again in the elevator by themselves. I would wait. Nancy had to chuckle as they took off in a run all smiles over such a small thing as a ride in an elevator. When they returned they were so excited to tell me about the nice lady that drives the elevator calling out each floor to help the shoppers find their way. Her name was Julia, and she had pretty short brown curly hair.

I don't know where the time had gone because it was already dark outside. We had not seen half the store, another reason to come back again.

As we boarded the trolley bus taking us to our beautiful rooming house, I couldn't help but notice the variety of travellers, from young to old. It was beginning to get busy with ladies wearing hats and gloves totting parcels in large shopping bags to put under their tree, I am sure. With the ropes of green garland decorating the inside of each wall in the bus, I thought how it was beginning to look more like the Christmas I had dreamed of.

As the bus began to roll along, we all managed to find ourselves a seat where we could see outside with a good view of the lights decorating the streets as our bus hummed along. I knew we must do this again, if only to dream of the many things that were not in our reach, but one day would be.

For some reason after having visited Woodward's beautiful department store, I just couldn't stop thinking about it. I knew that everything had been given an extra polish so that it would be the shiniest it could be. It was the most exquisite store I had ever seen. Oh, how I would like to be a part of it, but with a grade four education that was not likely to happen, but I could dream.

Several weeks later Nancy came knocking on my door later one evening. Before I could get there I could hear her calling me. Whatever could be the problem I worried as I hurried a little faster trying not to awaken Fritz. It had been dark out for some time already, few people go calling at this time. It must be important.

As soon as I opened the door, she pulled me into the hall whispering in a jumble of words I could not understand only that she was so excited she couldn't speak fast enough.

"Nancy, what is it?" I asked.

"Oh Emma. Just look what is in the paper tonight. It is just right for you."

"What? Let me see. You are shaking so much I can't read it." Then we both began to laugh like high school friends.

Leaning against the wall, I began to read, first once and then the second time. As I began to shake, I looked into her smiling face wondering how she could possibly know what I had been wishing for.

"Nancy, this is a job offer."

"Yes Emma. Read further. It is at Woodward's. I saw that dreamy look of awe in your eyes when we were walking through the store. You looked like a young girl in a make believe store as you walked through the clouds daring to wish on the first star you would see. You must apply for it. You will make more money than Nola can pay you to bake bread. There is nothing there that could be as hard as you have always worked. Think about it tonight. To-morrow we will talk. I will help you because I know you want to work there. You will make a perfect clerk. I know you will."

With that she turned around in her pretty slippers of blue, and headed for her suite leaving me standing there wondering what all had just happened. My knees suddenly felt weak. I had to get myself back into our suite before someone came home and saw me sitting on the floor with nervous tears running down my cheeks in the top hall. They would ask too many questions.

Morning came before I was able to close my eyes. There were just too many things going through my mind to make room for sleep. Now I began to wonder what I would say at the bakery when anyone asked me how come I looked so tired. Maybe they won't ask.

More than ever I kept to myself all day. During the noon break, Harold asked me if I was alright, but left me to my thoughts as soon as I said yes through a forced smile. I had now made up my mind.

The following day I brought the ad from the

paper with me in my purse as well as two dimes. One for the telephone call, and one should I have dropped the first dime. Nancy and I had discussed what I should say when I made the telephone call that could make another big change in our lives.

After supper I had taken Fritz and Katrin with me for a casual walk while I surveyed the nearby shops for a telephone. They had no idea what I was up to. I would not think of making the call from Quality Bakery. Not only did we not have a telephone at home, but it was too late when I returned at the end of my work day. The store would already be closed. Harold had told me to look near the Funeral Chapel. He was sure there was one there that would give me some privacy. He was right.

With every bone in my body shaking I made the call the next day during my lunch break, praying the right person would be there. He was, but all I got was an appointment for Saturday afternoon to speak with him. It would cost me bus fare that I did not wish to spend on just myself and a couple more nights of no sleep. I knew I had to take the chance. This could be the next step to a better life for my children.

I did not wish to think of the many applicants this soft spoken gentleman has had. I needed to think positive. I would have to convince him that this was a job that I both needed and could learn. I would not try to deceive him that I already knew how to do something that I didn't, but rather that I could learn. I would tell him how I made clothes over for my family without a pattern just using my instincts. Wasn't that a good start?

Saturday finally came. Arrangements were made with Mr. & Mrs. Smith to keep an eye on Fritz and Katrin. They kept assuring me they would be fine, that was the day I had planned to bake cookies she said. I wasn't fooled one bit but I was ever so grateful.

As I sat alone on the bus wearing my only hand-me-down suit with my well worn dress shoes that I had had for as long as I could remember, I tried to focus on the passing shops with the traffic whizzing past to help ease my nervousness. There was so much to see and yet my mind could only think of one thing, my interview.

When I exited the bus my eyes fell on this massive store called Woodward's Department Store in Vancouver. Would I actually be able to work in such a grand shop? I must give it my very best trying to sit up straight, crossing my ankles to look ladylike, and keeping a friendly smile on my face. I began to wonder if my dark blue suit was suitable for this job but it would have to do. It was my best. It was also too late now to do anything about it. It was what I had.

A half hour later I was making my feet carry me back to the bus stop on the further side of Hastings Street. First I moved one foot, then the other. They still felt as though they were made of rubber. I was so excited I couldn't think. Had I really gotten this job? The kind man said I did. Already I don't know what he looked like. I can't remember his name. I would start in two weeks. I would work in the shoe department. I would help customers find just the right size and style for them. I would keep the shelves well stocked and tidy. Someone will show me how to use the foot pad with a built in ruler for measuring. They will also show me where the chart is. I will be fine. I will make more money to live on. So many things to remember. Slowly but surely my dreams are happening, but I feel like my feet are on moving ground. Will I be able to do this job that will make our life better?

My first day on the job passed like a whirlwind in a prairie storm. There was people coming and going all day long. It seemed everyone was in need of a new pair of shoes. No one knew what size shoe they wore. Many seemed to think I could tell by looking at them. While I thought they all had big feet, I smiled at them as I did my best to find just the right pair, most of all they needed to leave feeling happy with their purchase.

At the end of the day as I was tidying up the display counters, this same tall man wearing a dark blue suit and shiny shoes came over to me. Oh no! Is he going to let me go, I wondered.

Not at all. First he complimented me on a job well done. He had someone keeping an eye on me all day and I didn't even notice. I was too busy, and now too tired. Then he said when I arrive in the morning, I was to report to the drapery department. Same procedure as this morning, whatever that was. It seemed as though that had been a trillion hours ago. Could I even remember?

It was only a few weeks later that I knew that

I had found my place in this prestigious store. I was so happy I couldn't stop smiling all day. I had never seen such beautiful material much less sewed with this heavy material called drapery fabric before. It was new, never having been used before for something else. I loved the feel of new fabric in such an array of colours and patterns. My first days there, my co-workers willingly gave me some assistance in measuring the fabric to be sure when the customer got home they would have just the right amount. It was fun for me to picture their windows looking bright and cheery.

That evening when I arrived home, Mrs. Smith greeted me as I stepped through the front door.

"Looks like you had a good day. Now I am just going by the smile on your face," she commented in her usual cheerful way. "Am I right, Emma?"

"Yes, you are right. I know there will be days that I will have to deal with difficult customers, but I will try to remember how fortunate I am to have this job. It is like a gift from heaven.

Today I had a lady that could not speak English. She couldn't even explain which room the curtain was going to be for. After I took her on a walk through the many bolts of different kinds of fabric, her face suddenly lit up as she pointed to a light-weight fabric in a pretty floral of different shades of blue.

My next idea was to point out different panels displayed on the walls depicting ideas for the rooms in a home. When she spied the one she was going to make, she began to point. Her kitchen. Now I knew how much fabric she would need, providing the measurements on her paper were correct.

As I watched her leave slowly making her way to the elevator, I breathed a sigh of relief. I felt that I had done my best to have a happy and satisfied customer, one that would be back again."

"Emma, you will make a fine employee. You have the heart for it. They will be so happy they hired you."

"Thank you Mrs. Smith. You are so kind," as I slowly made my way to the stairs.

I would come home to find Fritz and Katrin playing a game, usually checkers that Mrs. Smith had loaned us. They were accustomed to being inside with little to do but roll around on the floor pretending they could see all the stars as they described each one and which one was the brightest. Katrin still said that the one that sparkled the brightest was her friend in heaven. Everyone in heaven was her friend according to her. With her imagination she would give them names whenever asked. She said it was because someone should remember them so I will. I thought that was a nice thing to do.

One day I was busy doing my housework while Fritz and Katrin were helping along when Mrs. Smith called up that there was someone at the door to see us. Having no idea who it could be, I hurried down the stairs with two pairs of feet following close behind.

When Mrs. Smith opened the door wide I was shocked to see Floyd and another man standing there with only the screen door between us. I began to shake. My limbs were trembling. Katrin and Fritz pushed past me to get to the screen door that I was now holding shut as they shouted, "Hi Daddy, Hi Daddy!"

The next few minutes seemed like total chaos to me. Floyd was shouting at me to let him in while I was saying to wait a minute. Then Mrs. Smith stepped forward.

"Just a minute everyone. No one forces their way into my home," said Mrs. Smith in a no nonsense tone.

"Floyd. What do you want?" I asked. My heart was pounding but I tried really hard to sound calm and in control.

"I just came to get my kinner. I am going to take them home to the farm where they belong. Emma, you should come with me. We had a good life."

"No Floyd. We are not going back. We were barcly surviving. Fritz and Katrin need to go to school. Here they can do that. They are going to school every day during the week. They are healthy and happy."

"They have had enough of school. I can teach Fritz all he needs to know to run our farm. You teach Katrin to cook and sew. She will marry a farmer," said Floyd in a voice that was beginning to falter more by the second.

"Floyd. I am not going to discuss this in front of them any longer."

"Let them come out here so I can hug them for

a few minutes."

"No." I could see the other man was ready to step forward and grab them, especially Katrin. She would have been the easiest to pick up.

I decided it best to not answer further. Fritz and Katrin had gone inside with Mrs. Smith to her kitchen for milk and cookies. She had not said anything, just put her hands on their shoulders and ushered them in. They were safe. No one messes with Mrs. Smith.

After having seen Fritz and Katrin going inside with Mr. & Mrs. Smith, Floyd and I agreed to meet at Bill's Cafe on Kingsway at two in the afternoon the following day. With that I turned and closed the door.

I felt like I was ready to crumble into a big pile on the floor. I knew I had to at least sound strong. I had heard Mr. Smith say to Mrs. Smith that they should not be involved. Tell her to take her children somewhere else I am sure I heard him say. I also heard her reply. It went something like no way. A mother needs to do what she feels she has to for her children.

Putting on a brave face, I went inside their suite firstly thanking Mr. Smith for letting us live in their home. I told him how much I appreciate the comfort they have brought to my children and I. With that, he just nodded saying something I really couldn't decipher.

I walked into the kitchen to see Mrs. Smith chattering to my children. I knew she was doing her best to make them feel a little less sad. Bless her heart. I firstly asked them how the cookies were. Just like they had been taught, they both said they were good. When they finished their milk saying thank you, I suggested we go to our place. For the first time they seemed too happy to leave. They did not need to be coaxed. I felt so bad but could not go back on what I knew in my heart was the best for them and their future. If I didn't stick with my plan, there would not be another chance.

The following afternoon wearing our best we entered the cafe. Floyd and this other man, who I still did not know who he was, were already there sitting on stools at the lunch counter watching for us to enter.

This time they hung back. They were not eager to rush to their dad. I had not said anything at all about the situation. I am sure they talked to each other about it all morning while I was at work.

I had always known that they both loved their dad to no end just as he loved them. There was no one that could deny that, not even me, but then I didn't want to.

Floyd was a gentle man filled with patience and understanding for them from the time they were babies. I remember him having said, some years back, that a parent would give their life for their children. He would watch them play or work with a smile of pride on his face. Whenever he was complimented on them, his smile spread from one side of his face to the other. Then when we got home he told them how proud he was of them. He was a father that taught with love and kindness. Many times I wished I had had his patience. I didn't. It was Floyd that sat up all night on a hard kitchen chair holding Katrin in his arms while she cried from the burn on her arm received by falling against the hot space heater.

After greeting them with arms spread wide to take them into a big hug, he kissed them both many times. I know it was not to wear me down, but truly for his children. They cautiously responded.

I seated my children at a table away from the door. After asking me if he could please treat them to an ice cream followed by my yes, the waitress asked them which colour they wanted. When she brought them each a big dish of ice cream with sauce on top, one strawberry and one vanilla, I could see her heart breaking for them. She already figured out the story.

The strange man took a seat at a table between them and the lunch counter. My heart was pounding with fear that he would try to take them making the day that much more dramatic. Time for another quick prayer.

Please Lord, be with me and my children. Keep them safe. Amen.

There was only one other couple in the Cafe at the time. They were both engrossed in a conversation that seemed to make them laugh until the tears rolled down their cheeks. The waitress was a middle aged lady with dark hair wearing a white uniform with an apron over her dress. Perhaps it was just my mind, but it did seem that she kept looking from them to me and back again. As she did her best to do her work and not eavesdrop I knew she heard way too much.

Then came Floyd's first question. "Why did you run away with the children?"

"I did not think there was any other way. I had been telling you for a long time that we were barely existing, near starvation. The children were not receiving the schooling they should have. I want them to have an easier life."

"What is the matter with our life? We do not need anything more."

"Floyd. We do. We cannot expect to receive parcels from my sisters for ever with clothing their family no longer wears. We don't even have a radio or a pump for the well. It is just too much. I will not do it any longer when I cannot see it getting better. The winters are too harsh. You could be out here with us."

"No! I am a farmer and I have a farm. We will not leave."

"Then Floyd, you leave but do not return here, today, tomorrow or any other day."

"Emma, I need you there. I cannot do all the farm work by myself. Please come back with me."

"No Floyd. I am not going to do that."

With that I turned taking Fritz and Katrin by the hand as we walked out of the cafe. We walked back to our home in silence without looking back.

From that sad day forward I worried more and more about having to leave Fritz and Katrin alone while I went to work. Mrs. Smith suggested that she keep a discreet watch on them. She would take note of when they arrived home and where all they went if I could just come up with a way to have them come into the house frequently for some unknown reason. She felt the same as I did. I could not openly say I was afraid of what their dad would do. They loved him, and rightly so. Anything he did would be what he felt was for their good. There we did not agree.

While at work my mind was so full of customers coming and going that I barely had time to worry. It was when I was riding the bus with nothing to do but listen to the hum of the traffic going by that all things came to mind. I barely noticed the weather. Some days it was raining and dreary, some days the sky was a bright clear blue with tiny wisps of floating clouds. Anything was better than the deep freezing snow with the wind whipping it around you. For now I had too many other things going through my mind to make weather an important issue. We were warm and safe.

A few months later I received a raise in my pay. Such a wonderful surprise, and a much needed one. As I sat one evening after they were in bed, I looked over my income and my expenses. I needed to move. I would need to ask Nancy for her newspaper after she has finished reading it. There was always row upon row of places to rent. My needs will make it a little difficult. They would need to remain in the same school. There will need to be a bus stop reasonably close for when I come home from work in the dark during the dreary winter months. Then I will need a galvanized bucket on a long thick rope full of luck.

It was not too long after that I read of a small house for rent not far away. It was a small old house with a crab apple tree in the back yard. Their school would be a half a block from home. It had an upstairs with four small bedrooms. One bedroom could be accessed from the back stairs.

Nancy suggested that perhaps Jack could rent it from me. He worked nights so therefore when he slept during the day we would all be away. This may not be ideal but it would work, at least for a time. There would be a familiar face for the while until I came home from work. They would be safe.

After settling into our new home, Jack thought we all could take the bus to Lynn Valley in North Vancouver one Sunday afternoon. The weather was pretty much ideal for a walk outdoors. Nancy suggested we walk across the Lynn Canyon Suspension Bridge taking in the beautiful sight of the large Douglas fir trees surrounding the deep canyon as the bridge bounces and sways from side to side. It is a 50 meter high bridge that stretches across a beautiful canyon of raging waters rushing to get to the bottom, water falls tumbling down that sparkle in the sunlight, and pools of clear blue water swirling around and around. Making it even better is the free admission. Just leave it as one found it was all that was required.

With many walking trails in the park, the most famous is the Baden-Powell Trail from Lynn Canyon to the base of Grouse Mountain. It was named after Robert Baden-Powell, Lord Baden-Powell, the founder of the world Scouting Movement.

The walk is rugged but the trail is well maintained. It is about forty-eight kilometres long going from west to east as it winds through the heavily forested area.

As we stood looking at the map describing the trail, all we could think of to say was WOW! Just thinking about a walk like that made me tired. I suggested to Fritz and Katrin that should they ever have the opportunity to one day do even a portion of the trail they should. For now they felt they had walked through enough big trees already. I couldn't even assure them that there were no wild animals in that bush. I did promise them that one day we will come back wearing better shoes for walking. Then we will climb down the bank after we have crossed the bridge until we can walk on the rocks through the trickling icy water. Somehow I don't think the climb back up will be as much fun but we will discuss that later.

As we rode home on the bus I asked if anyone had noticed that the crab apple tree was nearly ready to burst into bloom. Since no one answered with a yes I began to tell them what a lady at work told me about her tree. Ours should be much the same.

I could already smell their fragrant springtime blooms that will soon be open for all to enjoy. Their distinctive clusters of five petals in each blossom with yellow stamens in the centre are a rich deep electric red attracting small singing birds. Nancy added that it has a great umbrella shape just right for sitting under in the hot summer sun to keep cool. She added that by the time the fruit is ready to pick to eat and can, their leaves will be turning to show their fall colours before they drop to the ground below.

"You know Katrin, they are sour tasting," she said.

"As sour as the rhubarb from our garden?"

"Yes, about that. They are hard too. You will see."

With that, we all fell into a time of relaxed silence. No one wished to touch the subject of our garden on the farm, least of all me. Then there had been too much excitement and walking to encourage conversation. As we each sat back savouring our memories of the day, we were stirred by the bus driver's call that we had reached our stop. We were back, well a couple more blocks to walk first. I think I can make it I thought as I struggled to my weary feet.

Nancy remained on the bus that would take her a few blocks closer to her home. I am sure her feet were sore and tired too so we bid her a goodnight as we went our way.

Jack went to the stairway that would take him to his room as we went to the back porch to enter into our kitchen. Just like on the farm, there was no need to lock the door. I do think there was a Skeleton Key left for us in the cupboard when we arrived. Fritz suddenly began excitedly scrambling to get to a box that was waiting for us just outside the door. I was too shocked to say anything. Who would leave something for us?

Before I could say anything more, Fritz and Katrin had carried the box inside setting it on the table. As I too peered into the box, I couldn't believe my eyes. It was filled with tins. They did not know what the tins could possibly hold and I was afraid to think.

As though I was moving in slow motion I picked up first one tin and then another examining it from top to bottom. Then one side all the way around to where I started. Whoever was so kind? This is like a gift from heaven. Before I could explain I sank onto a chair to keep myself from collapsing onto the floor.

"Mom. What is this stuff?" asked inquisitive Fritz.

With barely enough breath to breathe, I said, "The round tins are filled with salmon. That is a delicious expensive fish, not that I had ever tasted it before. The other tins are filled with Spam. That is meat that is made of pork shoulder meat. Pork is a city word for pig. I wonder who was so generous to give us this food?"

"So which one are we having for supper?" asked Katrin.

"Well, how would it be if we have salmon. That is the type of fish in the round tins. I will cook some potatoes and carrots to have with it. We will have the Span tomorrow night with some pork and beans. How does that sound?"

"Sounds yummy. Will there be fish eggs in there too?"

"No, this is only a part of a very big fish, but it will taste really good. Now you two need to put the rest away into our cupboards. It will be easy to find a spot."

Chapter Six

As spring was rolling closer to summer, I made a conscious effort to meet the parents of the neighbour children mine had become friends with. Why had I waited so long? Was I really afraid they would be judging me? Well, so be it. I must continue to think of my children first.

As I dared to think back to our life on the farm, I could see in my mind the snow that still remained on the ground during this time of the year. As it began to slowly leave us, we were left with a muddy road, a field with too much water, and a garden that was so deep in water the children would take the water trough out to ride in a boat before taking it back in to the corral for refilling with fresh clean water for the animals.

As Wednesday was my day off I was outside in the morning hanging the laundry out to dry in the fresh air when I heard a friendly voice call, "Hello neighbour."

"Good morning," I replied in as cheerful a voice as I could. I really did feel happy to see her but I was nervous all the same. From somewhere my mind managed to tell my feet to move towards the fence that separated our back yards.

"My name is Emma. I am pleased to meet you."

"Me too. I am Ida. My husband is Luke and that red headed kid your son plays with is ours. He's Ben."

With that I had to laugh which brought a pretty smile to her face. I felt an instant liking to her. I knew now we had a good neighbour.

"Well, you have probably seen my daughter Katrin around," I said.

"Oh yes. Ben said she is in his class at school. He says she is very shy and quiet. He thinks she is very smart."

After a couple more minutes of idle chatter, I explained I would have to excuse myself as this was my day off leaving me with much housework to do.

After Fritz came home from school, I asked him about Ben.

"So Fritz, what do you and Ben do when you hang out?"

"Nothing much. He just shows me around the neighbourhood. That's all."

"Soo, does Ben have a slingshot too?"

"Uh. Yah."

"Fritz! Don't you answer me like that."

"Sorry mom. Yes he does."

With that Katrin came into the room so I thought they both may as well get straightened out at once. There is no need for bad manners, not even in the city. They picked up slang so quickly upon coming to the city that it amazes me.

Saturday mid morning we were all busy doing our inside chores to prepare for the coming week when we heard the clip-clop of horses' hooves. For a moment we looked from one to the other in disbelief. That sure does sound like horses I thought.

We all hurried to the front window to be sure it wasn't our imagination. There before my eyes were two brown horses with shiny coats pulling a wagon filled with fresh vegetables as they slowly made their way along the city street. A man in his work overalls held the reins as he walked alongside the wagon.

He brought back memories of my sister and I going to town as young teenagers to sell the extra vegetables from our Mother's garden. Oh how Mother would love to see this if only to dream of what could have been. Then my mind went to Mary awakening a whole new bank of memories.

At times I find myself thinking of Mary. How good it would be to have my friend near so that we could share our feelings just as we had done years before. Every once in a while Katrin asks about Ashenee reminding me how much she likes her beaded head band. She wonders if Ashenee still has her hankie she had so lovingly embroidered for her.

Sometimes I notice she has taken her beaded headband from her treasure box just to look at it while she gently touches the beads with her fingers. She loves that headband. I am so happy that Mrs. Smith was able to give me a cardboard box that she no longer wanted to save. A pair of blue gloves had been inside for her birthday several years earlier. Now it's perfect for Katrin to be encouraged to treasure some special things as she goes through life. I placed a hankie in the bottom for her that I had embroidered in soft pinks and blues. She has as well a pretty box as a remembrance of Mrs. Smith.

While I still try to have hope that one day we

shall meet again, I know that is highly unlikely. Their tribe is not known to leave the Northern part of Saskatchewan. It is where their people are. But maybe, just maybe it will one day happen. There is no harm in wishing, and so I shall. I shall not be returning to Saskatchewan.

I frequently think of Floyd's visit at the Rooming House. I still feel bad that he was so angry when we parted. I cannot imagine how difficult it would be to loose your children from your life. If only he could have understood just how poor we were with barely a hope for tomorrow. That land will never grow anything but dust and stones. I still find it difficult to understand why he thinks his children should not have an education for an easier and brighter future.

Many times as I ride the bus, I think of our friends Marvin and Bertha. We had become so close to them. I was so appreciative of Bertha. There were times when I felt so alone in the world her friendship filled with kindness and understanding seemed to pull me through giving my spirits a new lift.

Then there was Imogene, and the Farmers, and not to be forgotten my dear friend Mr. Bosch. I must never forget them or take for granted all they have done for me. These people with the always kind and generous heart cannot be replaced. This reminds me, I must not prolong visiting my friend Harold. Perhaps next Wednesday when the store is closed I will visit during his lunch break. It seems so easy as we begin a new chapter in life with new things to do and new friends to drift away from those that have stood by us.

It seemed the week passed by me rather slowly. It has been raining most every day with a dark grey sky looming overhead which meant they were indoor days. These were evenings after work that I did some extra mending and sewing sitting in the warmth of a brightly lit kitchen. I began to take apart worn sweaters that no longer fit anyone for remaking into a warm sweater for each of us during the coming winter just like I had always done. I was years past being too proud to accept hand-me-downs. They were life savers.

When my day off came once again, I hurried through my housework, changed my clothes and made myself a sandwich to eat with my friend Harold. I was so excited to see my previous work mates that I found myself checking the clock every few minutes just to be sure I wouldn't be late.

As I neared the back door Nola came out to place something in the garbage.

"Nola, Nola," I called to her.

"Hello Emma. Good to see you. Is that your lunch bag you have with you?"

"Yes. I hoped to join Harold during his break."

"Well, why don't you just go in the little back room and wait for him. I will make sure he is there in a couple minutes." With that she abruptly turned and walked back into the Quality Bakery without another word.

It was as though I had just been gone for a few minutes. Everything in its place and a place for everything. I decided to stand leaning against the wall that had been painted a fresh white instead of sitting surveying the room as well as into the Bakery. It was still as spotless as it had been the first time I saw it, and just as hot. I did not know if he has started sitting on the stool instead of the bucket. I hope so.

When Harold walked in he wore a sombre face with a slight shuffle as he walked. Not his chipper self. All I could say when I saw him was "Harold. Oh Harold." I knew life was not dealing him a good hand. He wore the same clothes he had always worn, but he was not the same man.

Within seconds he threw his arms around my shoulders, "Oh Emma. Oh Emma. You came back my friend. It was so good to have you to talk to."

"Sit down Harold. Tell me how you are doing as you eat your lunch. I brought myself some lunch too. Just like old times." I tried to laugh a little just to lighten his heart the way it was when I first met him. I could tell by the dark circles under his eyes that he was carrying a heavy weight on his shoulders. It could only be Huey.

He sat on the bucket motioning for me to sit on the stool. I knew it would do no good to urge him to sit on the stool so he could rest better. That is not what a gentleman should do, and he was a gentleman.

"How is it going with you Emma?"

"Pretty good. I have had a raise making it a little easier. We will get by. There are days that I feel as though I do not know what I should do. I feel as though I am walking on a rocky road. I know I must and will push forward. But more important, tell me about you."

"I might as well get to the point. It is Huey. They came after him again. That is the three big thugs that came for him before. Huey and I gave them all the money we had saved for them but it still was not enough. Huey has been working one full shift and then another half shift at the warehouse just to save money to pay them off. They wanted the rest right then. We had no more. I begged them to be patient. We were trying to pay them back using every penny that we did not absolutely need to live.

Just when I thought they were going to leave one fellow hit me across the face knocking me to the ground. Before he turned on Huey he kicked me in the back. His other partner in crime was now holding Huey with one arm around his neck, the other holding his arms tight behind his back. As Huey repeated over and over to leave his Pa alone the thug that had been holding me began to punch Huey in the stomach watching him double over until he began to spit up blood. I knew they were not going to kill us, they still wanted us, but for us it would have been better to have it end. The beatings they gave us were as important to them as the money they wanted to recover. It was about power. This was their territory."

"Oh dear. I am so sorry. Have you talked it over with Huey about going to the police? Sometimes there are troubles we just can not solve by ourselves. There must be some help out there."

"Yes. We have talked and talked mulling it over and over time and again. The end is always the same, a no. He feels it will be even more dangerous."

"I thought I remember Nola saying that they were in jail serving time for another offence which was to keep them behind bars for a long time. What happened with that?"

"They have a hotshot lawyer, paid for with dirty money that was able to find a loophole in our law. The police had no choice but to release them. Frank says these thugs are part of a much bigger and stronger gang. They look after each other. It seems that jail time is a short visit for them. They have been in many times before. Each time the police think they have a good case against them, then dirty money seems to surface and they run free.

They have been accused of murder several times before, but there has never been enough strong evidence to put them away. It has just been fortunate that the police have been able to arrest them as it is without a blood spill. These guys just laugh at them. They have no fear.

I don't know Emma. Maybe Huey is right. It could be much worse for us than it is now. My gut feeling is that Huey and I shall never be free. I even thought of us moving to some far away country that we could just get lost in the crowd, but I don't know where that would be or how we could get there. Even if I did find a way to leave those countries are dark skinned people, mostly of Spanish ancestry. I think we would stand out in the crowd. We are too white to blend in. I will not put any of my friends in danger trying to protect us."

"I don't know what to say or think. This is very serious. I have very little experience in city life, but I think this is something that is way over your heads. Have you asked Frank what he thinks you should do? He would have a better feel for this than me."

"No. I am too scared and ashamed to go to him again. He has already helped Huey find a job. I am afraid that if he knows there is more trouble he will let him go. He needs this job. Huey says he is working really hard to keep it. I feel I can believe him."

"I know your break time is about over so I shall have to leave. I am so sorry that I cannot help you."

"Oh Emma. You did help me. Just having a friend to talk to meant so much. Please come back again whenever you can. I will talk to Frank."

With that I turned and slowly walked home carrying a heavy weight on my shoulders for my friend that had been so kind to me. If only someone could help them. I know they are good people doing the best they can in a tough world.

That evening after Fritz and Katrin had settled down inside the house for the remainder of the evening, I decided it was time to tell them of Huey. They had already met Harold. He was without a word from them, their favourite of all my new friends. He was quiet spoken with a soft gentle voice. I knew without saying who it was they were reminded of. Somehow I wanted to impress on their minds the dangers of city life.

Harold and I had spoken of this as we talked earlier in the day of his problems with Huey. It was his urging that I make my two aware of the dangers that can find them.

First I began by explaining, to the best of my ability, why I knew that I had to come to the city for a better life. I told them, without dwelling on it, how sorry I was. While they both sat motionless, I felt they understood that part but wished they could have it all. This was the time I told them how sometimes we have to make choices which won't always be easy. I am sure it was not an easy decision for your dad to leave here to go to the farm without us. I do know he loves you both very much. We must remember that is likely what he feels is the best. Neither one looked at me as they listened while they stared at the floor keeping their tears intact.

"I hope one day you will both understand what it is like to be a parent giving up so much for your children," I said. "The best way you can make your parents proud of you is to grow up to be an honest caring adult. Do no one harm, help others in need just as others have helped you, respect everyone including God. Try your best to follow His commandments and do His will."

We spent the next while discussing the friends they had made through church and school as well as in our neighbourhood. I found it difficult for Katrin to understand that while she may choose wisely, some may want to be her friend that could possibly lead her down the wrong path. She is known to instantly like everyone that wants to be friends with her. Immediately Fritz said, "Like that big mouthy girl in your class. She is trouble. You know, the one with the funny teeth."

Oh dear. Up until that comment came out, I was proud of him for cautioning his younger sister. All I could say in that quick moment was, "Perhaps she is trying to lead you Katrin. Be nice to her, but let yourself be drawn to your other friends. Include her, but do not be lead away. Her teeth have nothing to do with it. Beauty is on the inside." By the time I came to inside they were both speaking in unison with me. Guess they have heard me say that before.

Suddenly I felt Fritz's look upon my face. I knew just what he was thinking, but thought better of saying it.

"Fritz. It is my job to be sure that you both know about how harsh life can be while yet there is a different kind of harsh that we are trying to leave behind. I know you think that I have too many rules but that is my job too. There are always rules we must follow. This is my house, my rules."

As I rode the bus the next morning with dawn pushing the night sky away, I leaned my head against the cool rattling window as I looked off into the far beyond not really seeing anything but yet everything. I felt sick whenever I thought that just maybe Fritz could unwillingly end up being another Huey. A victim of circumstance.

I did not wish to frighten them, but I did want to instil in them how easily bad things can happen to good people, how this could easily cost Huey his life if not today one day further down the road.

That night I prayed, "Please Lord. Help me to not have made their life worse, in a different way, than it had already been. Keep them safe following your path. Amen."

One bright sunny day I had gone outside to the back yard to check on the laundry. With a nice gentle breeze blowing I thought it would be about time to be able to bring them inside. Everything should be dry.

As I stepped outside I could hear the chirping of the birds. This did remind me of the North. I knew by the sounds these birds were much smaller. They seemed to flit around not being aware of my presence. First they were on this branch, then in a moment they were in the next never seeming to sit still as they spoke to each other.

After taking a few moments to breathe in the warm fresh air, I began to remove clothes pegs from the clean sheets and pillow cases carrying them inside to put back on the beds for a peaceful night of restful sleep.

Usually I am in a hurry to get them all inside, put away and ironed if necessary so I could move on to other things. Today I just felt I really wanted to relax, wander around the back yard taking in the fresh air and sounds of the city before getting back to my chores.

Suddenly I was awakened from my beautiful

daydream to a voice calling my name. In a moment I knew it was Ida, my friendly but not overpowering next door neighbour.

"Hello Ida. Sorry about that. I was not ignoring you but rather enjoying the city air."

"Oh my," she said laughing. "I don't know if it is such good air, but the feel of one's own backyard is comforting. I like to do that too, especially when I am home alone. A few minutes of peace and quiet sooths the soul."

"For sure. So how are you and your family keeping?" I asked.

"We are all doing well. Keeping busy. How about you and your family? I wanted to ask you if your family likes pancakes?"

"Well, to tell you the truth I have never made them. We do like biscuits."

"Oh Emma. If your family eats biscuits you will surely like pancakes. We really like them. Luke suggested that maybe on Saturday night your family could come over for supper. We often have them for Saturday supper."

"That sounds like a real treat. What shall I bring?"

"There is nothing to bring just yourselves and your appetite. I think I will ask Jack too. Luke can talk his ear off for a while," she said as she began to laugh heartily.

As I returned to my laundry I thought how easily Ida laughs as though her life is a bowl of cherries all the time. Perhaps she just knows how to not show her troubles, if she has any.

The closer Saturday came the more excited we all became. I really did not know what to expect so all I could tell my family was that they were being so very kind to us. All we needed to do was show our gratitude. Who knows, this could be something we will all just love.

The next few days it continually played on my mind as to what I would take for a treat. Jack suggested I make something that we called a treat on the farm. Now that would be what, I thought.

Thursday evening it hit me. I could make Pigs Ears. I went over the ingredients in my mind, there were not many. My big concern began to shout in my ears. I do not have real good lard for deep frying. What ever will I do? Guess I will just have to do the best with what the city offers.

The next day during my break I rushed into the grocery department for lard. As I stood there staring at the shelf that held several kinds a clerk approached me.

"May I help you find something?" she asked.

"I was just trying to decide which kind of lard to choose."

"What is it your are planning to cook with it? Are you frying or deep frying?"

An instant feeling of mischievousness came over me. With my eyes on the shelf, I calmly said, "I am going to deep fry some Pigs Ears for dinner tomorrow night. On the farm I just used the lard from the pig when we butchered one." I had to really chew hard on my tongue to keep from laughing. City folk, they haven't lived.

She literally began to choke on her own breath. "Excuse me. Did you say Pigs Ears?"

I looked her straight in the eye as I calmly said, "Yes. They are delicious. I think I will take this one. Thank you for your kindness. Have a nice day." With that I turned on my heel taking some lard with me to the cashier as I chuckled to myself.

That evening as I was rolling the dough out Fritz and Katrin came inside.

"What is so funny mom?" Fritz asked as they looked at each other like I had just lost my mind.

It took me a few minutes to regain my control before I could repeat the story to them. They too laughed as they told me what a great one that is. I then had to have them promise they would not tell anyone as it isn't nice to make fun of someone else. I did know I would be sharing this shopping trip with Ida, not that I would tell Fritz and Katrin that.

I was just finishing making my surprise treats when Ida knocked on the kitchen door. As I dusted the flour off my apron I hurried to let my new neighbour in. I was excited that she had stopped over even just for a quick minute.

"Hello Ida," I said not trying to hide my pleasure.

"Hello Emma. I am sorry but I need to ask you if it would be alright with you and your family if you came for pancakes on Sunday night instead. A co-worker of Luke's asked him to change shifts for the day. It seems their little son is sick and needs to see a doctor. I hope you will still be able to come."

"Of course that is just fine with us. Don't give it another thought."

"Thank you so much. You know, it sure smells good in here."

With that she turned as she walked toward her home giving me a smile that said and just what are you up to.

That night I had one of the best night's sleep since we moved into the little house, and it was little but comfy. I woke in the morning with a light heart as I dressed for work. I had thought that when I moved to the city, and got a job I would have three or four dresses just for work.

As I pulled the curtain to the side of my closet I was overcome with emotion. I now had a closet just for myself. One that was bigger than the one all four of us shared in the Little Log House. There was room for my shoes on the floor. On a hanger hung my dark blue suit that I kept for Sundays. I had two print dresses to wear at home as I did my housework. Then there was two dresses one in blue with pale lime green leaves, and the other in black with tiny pink flowers. These I kept for work. They were both comfortable and washable. As they were a loose fitting I had no trouble reaching across the cutting tables. Again in my heart I thanked my sisters for sharing their dresses with me. A feeling of assurance that I had made the correct choice for our lives settled over me. I knew I was truly blessed.

As we knocked on the door for our much anticipated visit with the Mitchell family, I couldn't stand still. I was so excited to have made a friend for our family. Life was just getting better each day. Jack was already there enjoying an avid conversation with Luke as though they had known each other all their lives.

Ben quickly invited Fritz and Katrin to go with him to their basement. He was working on something that he knew they would really want to see. As I entered the kitchen with my large bowl in my arm, Ida was there to greet me.

As I handed my bowl to Ida, she carefully pulled the tea towel back to peek inside. "Oh yumm. These smell so good. What are they Emma?"

"They are Pigs Ears. I hope your family will enjoy them too. Now, can I help you with the pancakes? I am afraid I do not know anything about cooking pancakes."

"You will see real soon. Yes you can help me cook them but first I want to know about these yummy looking Pigs Ears. They do not look anything like the ones I have seen on a pig. However did you make them?"

"First I beat some egg whites until stiff. Then I mix in beaten egg yolks and salt. When that is mixed evenly I add flour. Just enough to make a soft dough. Then I knead it until it is a smooth dough. Roll it out onto a fairly large thin piece on a lightly floured counter. I cut it into squares. Slit one corner so you can pull the opposite corner through the slit. Finish by deep frying until a golden brown, and then sprinkle with a healthy amount of icing sugar.

This is a recipe that was my mother's. I only make it for a special treat. Too much work and time to make it more often. Besides, then it would not be a treat."

"I am so glad that you chose to make this special treat for us to taste. I can hardly wait to try them. Luke will like them and Ben eats everything in sight," she said shaking her head.

"So now let's get to the pancakes. Later when we do the dishes I will tell you of my shopping trip for lard, but since I told Fritz and Katrin they were not to tell others I will have to make sure there are no little ears around. It wasn't anything bad, I just don't want them to make fun of others."

After showing me her trusty fry pan that she uses for pancakes, she told me about the batter she mixes up. Her word of caution was to not have the batter too thick. Her family likes them thin and the size of her fry pan. With the precision of a professional, she poured batter into the pan flipping them over when the top was filled with small bubbles. Just as Ida said, the other side was a golden brown. When the underside is now brown as well, she slid it off the pan onto a large round dinner plate setting it in the oven to stay warm while she cooked more and more until there was a large stack. I wondered who was going to eat them all. I soon found out.

When Ida called everyone to the table, there was smiles all around. Katrin, who never says anything, was rubbing her tummy as she issued some oohs and aahs. Fritz and Ben did nothing to disguise their desire to dig into them. Ben showed them how he likes to pour pancake syrup over top making them swim. Oh my, I think they might drown. My two have never seen syrup like this much less had it been so plentiful. I was pleased to see them carefully pour a small amount minding their manners. Then Luke said they didn't do it right. I began to hold my breath. What had they done that I didn't notice. With a big smile he told them they just didn't take enough. He would have to show them how as he poured even more on their plates to make them taste even better bringing out smiles of wonder as their eyes grew larger by the second.

As we cleared the dishes from the table I thought I would never have believed that such a large stack would disappear so quickly. They were absolutely delicious.

As we washed dishes I told Ida about my shopping trip to the grocery store for lard. I was kind of relieved when she laughed and laughed about it.

"You know Emma. I would not have known what they were either, but I certainly would not have thought for one second they were the real thing. These are much better. We will enjoy them when we sit down with our second cup of coffee. I can see where they are very time consuming."

Later that evening I thought it was time for us to politely leave offering our thanks for a fun and delicious dinner. Our evening had been so delightful. It was easy to see we all enjoyed our time together over a simple meal.

As we made our way to the door, carrying my empty bowl, Luke announced that we need to do this again, real soon. We all heartily agreed as we bid each other a good night.

I went to bed with a feeling of contentment and pride of my children. They had made me proud.

After having at least a week of dreary rainy weather the sky turned to a pretty powder blue with not a wisp of white clouds to disturb it. The grass was a rich emerald green sparkling from a fresh wash of cool clear rain falling for a week to remove any traces of dust left there from our previous dry spell. Our apple tree was looking healthy as it prepared for a full crop of tiny hard apples.

Katrin had just asked me the previous night if we were going for a ride on the bus after church when Sunday rolls around again. I too had been wondering just what we could do or where we might like to go. Whenever I thought of it, I thought that the price of our bus fare made for a reasonable afternoon out. We always took our lunch with us. I tried to think of places we could visit that would be new to us. Since this is our new home I wanted them to know it. I wanted to remind them just how fortunate we were. I wanted them to see how much there was in the world to see and do, even just our tiny little corner of the world.

Like a call from the wind dear sweet Nancy came by the next evening asking me the same thing. She was missing our company. She worked in a jewellery store where like me, she waited on customers all day. We both enjoyed meeting so many people, but they did not replace the friendship of our friends. She needed some lady chat.

By one o'clock Sunday afternoon Nancy knocked on our door ready to go with her friend Edward beside her. I suggested that Fritz see if Jack was home and would like to go as well. Edward and Jack would be company for each other.

In a few minutes we were all set to leave with a route in mind. We had a light supper in her picnic basket that we all could share. What I didn't have, Nancy had. First we will watch the beautiful swans swimming around Lost Lagoon in all their grace at the base of the park. Hopefully there will be some peacocks strutting around showing off their beautiful tail feathers as they keep a watchful eye on the tourists admiring them.

Their iridescent tails fan out whenever threatened, to make themselves look bigger, displaying their eye catching markings in blues and greens. They have the most beautiful bright blue bodies that make their tails pale in comparison. The females nest for 28 days.

There is the famous Hollow Tree, a western red cedar that is said to be nearing 700 years old. This tree is the park's best known attraction drawing its visitors into its' trunk for that memorable picture.

Then if we have time we will see if we can spend a little time at the zoo watching the many animals lazing around for their visitors to admire them. They seem to lap up the attention as they show off their antics jumping from limb to limb all the while checking the crowd to be sure they are watching. Some tend to pose for a photo before leaping into the next branch. The last time we were there, we had very little time to watch the monkeys swinging on man-made trees, or the King Penguins as they waddle along with their short legs wearing their famous black and white tuxedos. While they glide through the water with ease, it appears to not be so as they move around on land with a side-to-side gait. This will make for a full day.

Chapter Seven

Fritz and Katrin were now going to start Confirmation classes at church in another few weeks. I had already discussed this with the Pastor that I was aware that Katrin was a year younger than Fritz. He insisted she would not be able to keep up with the class. "Do not worry," I told him. "She will easily keep up and then some with the others." After much persuasion he agreed to give her a chance, as he put it. If she began to fall behind she would need to wait another year. We agreed to meet after a couple months to discuss her progress. During the meeting they had both expressed their dislike for not being able to attend together. He didn't understand. As we walked home I told them it will be alright, wait and see.

The summer had started to close with fall beginning to settle in the air. Once again the leaves were beginning to change colour, some falling to the ground. It still was amazing to me that the grass was still green and healthy looking. We had had some rainy days. Sometimes they ran into each other for a week. I didn't mind. I knew it would not come down in the form of hail with a strong wind hurling it deep into the ground wiping out everything in its' path. It felt so good to not have to worry about our garden and crops being destroyed by things beyond our control. I would still have a pay cheque. We would still eat. Three times a day. They maybe weren't square meals, but we were not going to bed hungry.

I had made a new friend at work. Mildred was a petite bubbly lady with a friendly smile. She worked in the drapery department as I did, just not a clerk waiting on customers. I don't know exactly what she did but seems to be a lot of paper work, tallying of sales slips and so on. As we had our lunch break at the same time, we had an ideal opportunity to visit with each other as we rested our feet while we ate. She introduced me to the other ladies in the lunch room that worked in either the house wares department or the china department. Both seemed interesting but not nearly as much fun as the drapery department. I was happy right where I was. They were so delightful to work with. There were many others having their lunch at the same time, but these ladies seemed to be the ones Mildred knew. Lunch time was most often filled with happy conversations just like I needed. It always flew by much too quickly.

By now I had experienced this wonderful hectic day the first week of each month at this famous store, Woodward's. Everyone living in Alberta and British Columbia knew about it. It was beyond busy. It was so much work, but I loved it so much. A new and unexpected experience for me. I did not know about 'Sale' days anywhere before coming here.

It was called $1.49 Day. Every department in this large store had items on sale at this great savings. People lined up outside just waiting for the door to open to be one of the first inside to get first choice. All day Monday we had prepared our inventory for the next day when bedlam would break out. Sometimes in many departments there was pushing and shoving in order to get to the front of the line for that much coveted item.

Tony Antonias from neighbouring New Westminster, B.C. created a jingle that quickly became famous. People all over town could be heard chanting $1.49 Woodward's! $1.49 Tuesday! Men walked down the street whistling this catchy tune.

I shall always remember how I made so many friends in this large store not only in the drapery department, but in many other departments as well especially house wares. Another very special memory I shall never forget is the many times Charles Woodward walked through our department saying hello to each of us adding a couple personal words just for us. No one knew when he would visit, but everyone knew he would visit each of them as often as he was able. He was known to have a personal interest in his employees. I felt so proud to be a part of his Woodward's family.

The Woodward's chain was founded in 1892. This massive red-brick building filled the corner of Hastings and Abbot Streets with amazing window displays until 1993 when it became necessary to sell to the Hudson's Bay Company taking on a new look both inside and out.

There was also a smaller department store at the corner of 48th Avenue and Fraser Street called Honest Nat's. They were well known for their great year-around prices stocking a little of everything in this one floor shop.

I remember hearing on the radio of a men's store with a catchy commercial that went like this, Your haberdasher must be Fred Asher. Somehow it always made me smile even though I had never been inside. Today a haberdashery is just called a Men's Clothing Store, kind of plain I think.

That fall Jack suggested that he would meet me downtown Vancouver along with Fritz and Katrin at the White Lunch on Granville Street. Even when the streets were dark and dreary this sparkling clean restaurant drew an aah from passers-by during the winter months.

Inside it was brightly lit up with white flooring spattered with dark grey blotches, white Arborite table tops with fresh painted legs and chairs that matched. Paper serviettes sat in the centre between clear glass salt and pepper shakers with a sugar bowl and a vinegar cruet on each of the other two sides.

All over the city people talked of getting a milk shake for 15 cents, sundaes for 35 cents and a coffee for 5 cents plus fresh made sandwiches on fresh bread each day. More items were available just for the asking. Over the years their prices increased to cover their expenses like everywhere else.

It has been said that in 1937 the staff at all of their locations staged a six month strike and won for improved working conditions as well as higher wages. While the White Lunch boasted of having a rotating neon coffee cup sign, they closed their doors in 1970 much to the disappointment of their faithful customers.

This was the first time we had gone into a restaurant in downtown Vancouver. Katrin said she would never forget that delicious pink sundae. I am sure she hasn't.

That same week it was time for me to meet with the Pastor as to how my children were doing. As agreed I met him in the Chapel being sure to be there at the appointed time. When he entered wearing no sign of a smile, I began to get panicky. What could be wrong? As it turned out, he was just in thought.

When his smile broke out, he reached for my hand bidding me a friendly good morning. "Well Mrs. Ziegler, it seems you do know your children. Katrin certainly has no trouble keeping up with the class. Fritz however, needs to work harder in order for him to remain in class."

"Thank you Pastor. I shall get after him to stop staring out the window and do more studying. I will see that Katrin helps him."

Needless to say my conversation that evening was only half welcomed. Fritz was now a teenager with other interests that he was determined to follow, one was not Confirmation. With some strong words from me to the two of them, they could either study and pass or go another year until they can pass. As usual, he did some whining but agreed to apply himself. Katrin said she would help him with his studies but he had to put his feet on the floor, not the table.

I did remember to compliment them on how

they were earning some spending money. Fritz had a paper route and Katrin was babysitting. She was also helping with the housework and making meals. Sometimes they turned out very well, others not so good but she had to learn. One night she opened a can of pork and beans for supper. Instead of just warming them, she cooked them for about twenty minutes. They were very mushy but still tasted the same. Fritz ate his heartily saying how they were just fine, there was nothing wrong with them. His support for his sister made the beans seem perfect, and she had tried. Sometimes I wondered if he was so supportive because she had chores to do and he didn't.

I was beginning to see what city people had to say about living in a city. Life became routine just like on the farm but without backbreaking work. While the winter was a little on the cold side, it didn't compare to the winters in the North. Summers seem to be the same. Not near as hot and dry with lots of wind to blow the dust and dirt every direction. Most of all there are extremely few flies and mosquitoes. I will not miss those pesky insects.

We were still getting up on Saturday mornings, every few weeks, to find a box tucked in close to the back door filled with canned food. I am sure the whole neighbourhood must have heard Fritz hooting with joy as he carried it inside to set it on the table. Without it I am not so sure that we could have eaten as well as we did. There still would have been more than we had on the farm, but not enough to make their lunches healthier. Now there was something to put on their bread for lunch. It may have been sardines, canned fish or canned Spam, it didn't matter. It was all delicious. A can of Spam was enough for one supper and one lunch for the three of us. One day I will be able to purchase powdered mustard and some vinegar to make Mother's homemade mustard. While my mother grew her own mustard seeds to crush I never did. They just would not grow on our farm. Perhaps they were sending me a message.

Fritz and Katrin were still going to Dad's Cookie Window, as it was called, on Saturdays with a quarter to purchase a brown lunch bag of cookies. Perhaps this is what Fritz did not like about Confirmation. They had to wait until after class to go. No matter how I tried to ration them out, they never seemed to last a week. Maybe it was good that we had to do without a cookie for a couple days, but none of us liked it. We all missed our cookies.

It seemed that Jack was spending more time with our family. Of course, I was happy for the company. Having an adult to speak with made the evenings pass more quickly. Even with the radio on, the house seemed empty at times.

One evening he said he had seen oolichans for sale in a fish shop on his way home from work. If it was alright he would stop in tomorrow and bring some home for supper for us all. He promised to inquire as to how they were cooked as we had never seen such a thing. It turned out they were just like a larger sardine but oilier. We all decided we liked them, and were willing to have them again which we did as the years went on.

A few nights later there was a knock at the front door. It was already getting dark so as I hurried to see who was there. I couldn't help but wonder who would visit at this time of evening.

Even though I had never met him I instantly knew it was Huey. He was a younger version of Harold. As I led him into the kitchen I saw the battle scars on his forehead and cheek. I did not want anyone to draw us into this dangerous life, but how could I not offer at least a little help.

Finally he spoke in a soft whisper. "I know you are Emma. My dad spoke of you so many times. He spoke so highly of you that I thought you must be some kind of Heavenly Angel sent to earth to be a friend to us all. I know you are wondering how I found you. I followed you home from the bakery one day. I just had to know. I never planned to rob you or do you any harm. I just thought that maybe my dad may hide out here when it got too rough for him. I am so sorry I brought all these troubles on him."

I put my hand on his shoulder to stop him from rambling on any further. I needed to digest just what all he was saying. I felt he needed to slow down to catch his breath. As he spoke he was becoming more excited which made me a little nervous.

"First of all Huey, let me get you a glass of water," I said as calmly as I could.

"So Huey, are you afraid to go to your father's place for fear of the thugs waiting for you?"

"A little. I am not sure they are still looking for me, but then I don't know that they are not either. Frank said someone paid them the last of what I owed. They told him their business with me is over, but I really do not know if I can believe them."

"It looks to me like those scars on your head are not all healed up yet. They can not be from too long ago. Is that right?"

"Not really. I got infection in them so the druggist gave me a sample of some suave to put on it. It wasn't quit enough, but I thought it would do as I didn't have money to buy more. Guess it wasn't because soon after the infection came back. Now it is nearly better. I am still working for Frank. I put in two extra hours each day cleaning the yard and inside of the warehouse to repay him for his kindness.

I told Frank one day that I thought I should move away so they can't find me again. He said if they want to find you they will no matter where you go. I am better to be here where him and my dad are around. Guess he is right. I don't know.

I really do not want any trouble. I want to continue to build myself a life, be of help to my dad and not a burden. Besides I met a young lady one day. Her name was Hazel. I really liked her. I want to find her again."

"That all sounds good Huey. I hope you will be able to find her. So really, why did you come to see me?"

"I needed someone not connected to talk to. I wanted to thank you for being so nice to my dad.

He really is a great guy, you know."

"Yes, Huey. I know that. He is a great friend to have. I treasure that. Do you have a place to stay tonight?"

"Oh yes. I can stay with my dad. Not for too much longer though. Then I need to find my own place to live. Frank said he will help me find Hazel. I want to marry her, you know."

"That sounds so exciting. I wish you so much luck. Perhaps if you do leave again, you will keep in closer touch with your dad so he won't worry so much. That's what parents do you know."

After Huey left that evening I began to get ready for bed. I spent so much time wandering back and forth in the house not being able to concentrate on my task at hand that I accomplished nothing. By that time I really didn't know just what it was I thought I needed to do.

Lying in bed for a while trying to think of many other things to help me sleep, I decided I would just lay as still as possible with my eyes closed so that I could at least rest. After some time my eyes began to feel heavy. I drifted in and out of a light sleep again.

As I prepared for work in the morning I felt drained. I felt that I had not reached out to my friend Harold as much as I should have. So many people have helped me and my children to have made our lives so much better. Some still are. I am still grateful, and try to remind my children that we have a better and easier life because people have helped us along the way. They both translated that into the box of food that was periodically left at the back door.

That day shortly before it was time to punch the clock to leave for home, a senior manager came to have a word, as he put it, with us. Sometime during the day there had been a theft in our department. A display had gone missing from the wall, curtain rods and fabric leaving not a trace behind. Not one of us had seen anything. While it was no more my responsibility than anyone else's I couldn't help but feel that I had not been as alert as I should have been.

We had received a couple bolts of a nice quality fabric that was new out. It was in shiny pastels all sewn and ready to hang in someone's kitchen window over their sink. It was not the quality of fabric that would have been found in the ordinary working man's kitchen. The rods were a new brand that we had not carried before as they were more expensive. The thief knew what he wanted. He, or she, was not an amateur.

As I sat on the bus staring out the window as we rolled passed first one shop after another then turning into more of a residential area with scattered strip malls along the route, I found myself thinking of today's theft at work. If someone is so brazen to steal right off the wall with customers and clerks around would they perhaps go into our homes too. I have never given a thought to anyone not locking their doors, but began to wonder if since the children come home from school before me that just might not be a good idea.

I knew that somewhere in the house was a Skeleton Key for the kitchen door. Perhaps I should look for it and then use it. Tomorrow I will ask Mildred just what she knows about this kind of key. For tonight I will just trust that God will continue to look after us keeping us safe as He has done before.

After Mildred telling me that a Skeleton Key will work to open most doors I decided there was not much to do but, as suggested by Mildred, to find the key and leave it in the lock on an angle from the inside when we are in bed. This will prevent anyone, well most anyone, from pushing it out with another key. It is not much of a safety measure, but perhaps better than nothing. I was not worrying about anyone breaking in before so not much point in starting now. Even if I was, I cannot afford to have someone change the locks. Perhaps I will try speaking to the landlord.

One evening while Nancy was visiting she spoke of going to Chinatown with Edward. After telling us of the little shops in an array of colours selling many trinkets as well as lamps, vases and other decorative items Jack suggested that we make that an afternoon outing sometime soon. This sounded like an interesting and fun time. Again we would only need bus fare. It bothered me to think that my children would want to have a trinket to take home with them. This is one time that I cannot disappoint them.

When the big day came, the dull sky was over-cast with clouds looking like black smoke threaten-ing to rain but surely it will hold off until evening. We will be home safe and dry before then.

Chinatown is in the neighbouring streets of Prior and Powell Streets on the edge of downtown Vancouver. In spite of the weather being cool, this afternoon it was a hub of activity. The many small shops of bright reds with Chinese lettering in a gold colour displayed a life of another land with a foreign language distinguishing between the locals and the visitors. I am sure we stood out as a first time visitor. We had to drag ourselves away from one shop to visit the next which seemed to be even more interesting. I could barely begin to imagine what it would be like to live in China where ev-eryone spoke this new language. Mr. & Mrs. Wong from the Ritz Cafe spoke English to all their cus-tomers, but then we never patronized a restaurant when we went to town. For those that did, the Ritz Cafe was the only restaurant to choose from.

The sidewalks were busy with shoppers hur-rying from one shop to the other choosing fresh fruits, vegetables and fresh fish to take home for their supper. Fruits are common gifts. The tanger-ine and large orange is a prayer or a wish for good fortune. Sacks of rice, their main staple, are neatly piled on large tables. Ducks ready for the oven can be seen hanging in the markets. Fresh fish is very popular and considered a part of their daily menu.

There are different types and sizes of laughing Buddha's to choose from each with it's own significance and meaning as well as placement around the home. The different colours of the lotus flower in Buddhism hold significant meaning, each its' own.

Many people throughout the city make the trip to visit their special restaurant to dine. Mings and the Ho Ho Restaurant are two of the favourites advertising the best chop suey in Chinatown. Walking the streets was a safe and fun experience while the shops were open. After closing time the neighbouring streets were not desirable areas to be in, particularly after dark.

After wandering the streets for a few hours, it was decided that an ice cream cone would be the treat for the day. While Fritz and Katrin had each been fascinated with the Jacob's Ladder, they chose a candy bar from one of the stores that sold more items than they could take in. We were each able to take home with us many memories of a day filled with sights we had never seen before, but will savour for a lifetime.

It had begun to weigh on my mind as I rode the bus that when the next school year began Fritz would need to change schools. He would then be in grade nine. This meant that I needed to give some serious consideration to another move. One that would be good for the two of them.

After enjoying another pancake supper with Luke and Ida, the three kids went downstairs to do their own thing, as they called it, I mentioned this to Luke and Ida. Luke's face lit up. He said it wasn't that they wanted to see us move but understood with them growing and getting older, it was needed.

On his way home from work last week he had seen a sign of a house for rent with a lease to purchase option. It would be within walking distance for both Fritz and Katrin. They would be going to the same school not requiring a change of schools again until after grade twelve. Luke said he was just too happy to stop by on his way home from work on Monday bringing me whatever he could for contact information.

That night I went to bed again with feelings of mixed emotion. Would I be able to handle this? I must have asked myself this question at least a dozen times with no confident answer returning. I had learned enough of business while in the city to know that it is better to put my money into something that will one day give something back than to line someone else's pockets.

As I lay with eyes wide open once more, my tummy began to quiver every once in a while. Was this excitement or nervousness? Maybe I am getting into something that I cannot handle. Maybe I am just not feeling settled yet. Maybe it is a good thing to be a little cautious. Maybe I just need to trust my instincts once again. Maybe I just need to close my eyes and leave it to God to lead me. Too many maybes.

Chapter Eight

A few days later I was to meet with the owner in the evening. After Luke telling me how big a house it was I casually asked Jack if he would like to go with me. From what the owner told me, I thought it must have a suite upstairs that could be rented out.

I could hardly believe my eyes. To me it was huge. It was a large two floor stucco building on a big fenced in lot. While it was a long way from being a new home, it was well maintained. There was a back set of stairs that entered into a long hallway with a full bathroom just inside the door. There were two bedrooms, one connected to the suite while the other was near the back entrance. From the kitchen one could go out onto a large balcony that spread from one side of the building to the other.

The main floor was nicely laid out with a small mud room as one entered through the back door. It was large enough to store the washing machine, an ice box as well as ample room for outdoor coats and boots. The wringer washer was included.

From the kitchen one could access the stairway going upstairs. There was a telephone with a party line at the bottom to be shared by everyone in the house.

It certainly seemed like it would hold us all. Jack agreed. All I had to do was place a small advertisement in the local paper for someone wanting to rent the suite. Then I knew I could manage it.

The little comfy house we had been renting was heated from the sawdust burner stove in the kitchen. Sometimes when the children refilled the hopper they spilled some sawdust leaving it to be swept up. The oil stove we would now have would not be nearly as messy.

As I lay in bed waiting for the Sand Man to come I thought how I have come from a wood and coal stove to a sawdust burner and now to an oil stove. Maybe the next stove will be either gas or electric with a furnace to heat the house. At the end of the day, I was grateful for all that we now have.

Instead of closing my eyes I kept thinking of the new things this home will bring. That large Bing Cherry Tree made my mouth drool. By now I knew the fruit was a large dark red with a juicy flesh. Under the wide mass of branches was a bomb shelter, still useable. Now that was not something I had ever been searching for. I would need to plant some flowers in the front of it to disguise it from passing pedestrians. My first priority.

In the back of the yard next to the lane was an old, and I mean old shed that had never seen a spot of paint. It had to have been built from left over slabs from another construction project when the house was new. I am not sure if it held a tree up or the tree held it up, but together they stood looking as though they were determined to not collapse at any moment.

I was told the roof hardly leaked at all, just a couple small holes. Inside was a Walk Behind

Push Reel Lawn Mower looking as though it had mowed many a lawn. That would be just right for Fritz. There was even a lawn rake just waiting to be used. It too looked as though it had had much experience. They came with the house, free for the taking.

This well conditioned home stood tall at the top of a hill. It was a half block up from a busy street with bus stops going both directions. That busy street was 41st Avenue. Just a block away was a busy well run corner store. There we could pick up bread and milk should we run short. A few blocks up was the high school to which they could easily walk. One problem. Fritz could transfer there but Katrin would need to transfer to another elementary school to finish her grade, adding an extra school for her for just a couple months.

Just as I expected she was not happy and I couldn't blame her. Instead she chose to ride her bike to the school she had already made friends in. This would mean close to three miles each way, but she said she could do it, and do it she did with never a complaint regardless of the weather. She always just did it with no whining.

One Sunday afternoon Nancy came to visit. As she had promised to drop in for coffee one day, I was not surprised. It was her heavy heart that she could not conceal that I noticed within a few minutes.

As we sat at the table with our coffee she began to tell me of life in the Rooming House. Just as I would have expected, things have changed. How could things go so terribly wrong for such a sweet and caring couple I wondered.

Mr. Smith had not been feeling well for a while but like most men, he would not visit their doctor. There is nothing wrong with me, he would say. Along with his colour not being good, his energy had gone down and his appetite was waning. Apparently after a while Mrs. Smith told him she was making a deal with him, and he didn't need to agree if he didn't want to but this is what is going to happen.

"You will start moving around and eating all your meals, and I mean everything I put on your plate or I will have the doctor come here to see you," she sternly told him.

"No you won't," he adamantly replied.

"I will! Just you wait and see if I won't."

Nancy said she tried to not smile as Mrs. Smith told her the story. Well, I guess he did not want to do either so she called the doctor. When he showed up at the door Mr. Smith could be heard throughout the house, tenants and all.

Nancy said she was just coming home from work when all this ruckus started out. Since she had to wait a couple minutes on the front porch before she could get passed them to go up the stairs there was no way she could not hear.

Much to Mr. Smith's surprise the doctor said how he had better do as she said, and by the way reading the newspaper is not what I told you before about getting exercise. Then the doctor told him he would be back by the end of the week. If he didn't look any better he would be hauling him off to the hospital.

With that he turned and walked down the front steps giving me a smile and a wink as he passed by me.

"So what is the problem?" I asked.

"Well, the doctor had to return accompanied by a big strong orderly. Mr. Smith was told he could go with them to the hospital for a check-up or he could lay on the davenport right here on the porch while he did a complete check. Which do you want he was asked."

I had to laugh even though it is not a funny story, but when Nancy tells a story she puts her whole self into it. She can be very dramatic, and she loves drama.

Apparently the doctor won, and Mr. Smith went with them to the hospital. The end result was the tests showed that Mr. Smith was a diabetic, so now began the next battle. Poor Mrs. Smith. She is supposed to care for a sweet on the outside and stubborn on the inside husband. The first thing the doctor said was he no longer could have two spoons of sugar in his cup of coffee which he had three times a day. The candies had to go and the cookies needed to be limited to two cookies each week. This was just a start.

Nancy went on to say that things just seemed to be settling down throughout the house when the new tenant in Jack's room got much too loud. This has been slowly coming. He was told like the rest of us, when he moved in about the rules of courtesy to the other tenants which included noise. Mrs. Smith had no idea that he had such a drinking issue until of course it was too late. You know how sweet she is. He seemed like such a kind young man and perhaps he is but drinking does not bring out the best, she said to me. She felt just terrible having to ask him to move but she really had no alternative.

Now there is an older lady in that room. I think she is very nice even though she keeps to herself to a fault. The only problem Mrs. Smith has is that she forgets to turn the tap off in the bathroom sink. If she just didn't put the stopper in it wouldn't be so bad, but it has already run over twice leaving a mess for Mrs. Smith to clean up. There is also the worry of it ruining the floor covering and running through to the main floor. Otherwise she seems to be a great tenant. The rest of us leave our door open a tad bit to keep an ear open for running water. Since she cannot remember which day is her laundry day, Mrs. Smith goes up in the morning and lets her know.

Now your suite is another story. Sorry I am laughing, but it is kind of funny. They are a middle age couple, both working so are only home in the evenings. Now that should be no problem but they do seem to be night owls. About ten o'clock they seem to come to life for about three hours kicking up their heels as they dance to the music on the radio. I can hear them clapping and laughing as though there was a party going on in there.

Mrs. Smith spoke to them about this receiving

a promise to be more quiet in the future. The next night all is quiet. Then the next night it all begins again. I can lightly hear the music in my room, but I chose to tell Mrs. Smith that I never hear a thing. They really don't disturb me. It's a good thing that Mrs. Sprake is mostly deaf or for sure she would be driven out of her room. I am afraid that they will need to give them their eviction notice. It is hard to get someone in that is respectful to the rules.

Soon we were moved into our new grey stucco home. Not having gained a whole lot of possessions it didn't take long. I began to keep watch in the newspaper for anyone wishing to rent a small suite. Having no telephone until we moved in, I was not able to begin my search ahead of time.

After speaking with two couples, neither of which I felt comfortable sharing my home with I began to feel a little discouraged. Perhaps this will not be an easy task after all, but it did need to be a couple that would fit in with my family even though they had their own entrance and suite.

One evening just as we were clearing the table from our supper, a young couple came to the door.

"Is this the home that has a suite for rent?" the young lady neatly dressed in a pretty green dress under a brown coat asked.

"It is, but how did you know?"

"I sat beside a lady that appeared to be about your age on the bus today as I came home from work. She had dark hair with loose curls. We began to chat and I told her how I was looking for a suite for my new husband and I to live."

Without asking anything more I knew it was Nancy, but I asked anyway if she knew the lady's name.

"Oh sure. It is Nancy. I often see her on the bus. We generally just comment on the weather. I am so glad that today I sat beside her and took up a chat."

"Well," I said. "Why don't you come in so I can show the suite to you."

Firstly we looked at the kitchen which she just loved commenting on how clean it was. It was then that I remembered I had not asked her what their names were. "Rita and Pierce Child," came her gentle reply with a warm friendly smile on her face. Pierce just stood there with his hands behind his back and smiled. I thought how this man is either very shy or just doesn't speak. He too was well enough dressed. I tried not to stare at his hair but rather concentrate on how tidy and clean he was. He had light brown hair with a reddish orange shine to it. His head appeared to be covered in little springs that would not lay down.

They seemed ever so impressed with the sun porch off the kitchen telling me how Pierce will love to sit outside to read the newspaper. A few minutes later she said they would love to call this their home knowing how comfortable they would be living here. I had not noticed that they had discussed this together, but maybe there was a knowing look that passed between them that I had not seen.

After a few minutes to discuss the rent, when it

was expected to be paid along with the usual house rules I bid them a good evening. She would be back the next evening with Pierce to give me some money so I would be sure to hold it for them, she told me. My heart felt so much lighter just knowing that I was not going to have to ask made me feel that they will likely be paying their rent on time, no guarantees mind you.

Soon we were all settled in, both tenants and us. Katrin hopped on her bike each morning and headed off to school by herself. Fritz soon made friends with a couple boys in the neighbourhood helping him with his new school of a few hundred students. Next year Katrin would be able to join him at this school. However, her first year she would not be in the main building but rather in the Annex on 43rd Avenue which had received the nickname "The Barn". This school also separated the grade eight and nine students in that the boys and girls could not mix. First the boys had their lunch time in the cafeteria and then the girls. No mixed classes.

It wasn't long until I received another increase in pay again. Jack suggested that we go together and purchase a car he had seen for sale. It was a little older Ford four door in black and white but good running condition. Neither of us would be using it to travel to work. Since I wanted to visit the Okanogan orchards to see the fruit trees when they were bearing fruit, this sounded like an intriguing idea. I had been told we could go straight to the growers to pick our own fruit and tomatoes. Tomatoes were selling for $0.50 for a wood apple box filled. That would not take long to fill. Easy pickens!

For me life was good. I was feeling like I had made the right choice. Both Fritz and Katrin were doing well in school, getting the education I had dreamed of them having. By now they had both been confirmed in the Lutheran Church. Another dream that would not have been possible on the farm. Fritz was delivering newspapers that gave him some spending money. Katrin found new neighbours to baby-sit for. Me, well my job was doing well. I had learned so much. Slowly but yet quickly was working my way up in the department. I loved my job and those I worked with. We were not rolling in money, but we were certainly making ends meet much easier. There was no longer a surprise box waiting by the kitchen door in the early morning hours for us.

Our friendship with the Mitchell family remained busy and strong. We continued to enjoy the pancake suppers together with Ben and his red hair with a broad smile carrying their large fry pan on the bus whenever we were hosting.

Due to Nancy's health she was no longer able to join us on our excursions to Stanley Park. When I mentioned this to the Mitchell's they said they were just too happy to join us if we would have them. Of course we were delighted. Ben quickly promised to show us a Monkey Tree. As we all sat around savouring the taste of those pancakes, Luke began to tell us about this tree that we had never heard of.

Luke said it is native to Chile and closely related to the Norfolk Island Pine. The bark is fire resistant. He said it is also called a Monkey Puzzle Tree because it is a puzzle to the monkeys to climb up its whorls of spiny leaves often leaving the monkeys injured. As any fallen leaves are toxic to some animals, it is not a recommended tree for the home yard.

Soon a mild Sunday afternoon came. We had had several days of light rain leaving the grass a rich green. The trees and shrubs looked refreshed having been washed from the dust that had been settling upon them. The air smelled fragrant and light.

Like always, the Mitchell family knew which bus to catch so that we could ride together giving us extra time to visit as we enjoyed the sights together. Before I knew it Lost Lagoon was within my sight. The beautiful water fountain in the middle never ceased to amaze me with it's clear sparkling sheets of water falling in large drops into the mass of water that was home to the lazy swans.

As Ben led us along one well worn path turning onto the next we soon were in the midst of a forest of green trees. This next little path will take us there, Ben promised. He was right.

There before us stood this most beautiful but yet unusual looking tree reaching at least forty feet high with branches spread wide. Its dark rich green whorls enhanced its beauty. The pine trees and shrubs framing it made an amazing picture as it stood proud and tall for many years as though it was the centre of the forest, and king of all.

This time we found a comfy spot on the soft grass near the popular big stump to have our snack. Nancy had generously given her picnic basket to me bringing our thoughts to this great friend each time we visited her favourite park. This stump had been well climbed on for a number of years by the young people, our three no exception. This is where Fritz and Ben liked to sit to play cards thinking we had no idea what they were doing. Gee, could it be poker? Whenever Luke questioned them, the answer was an innocent no. He always left them with a stern reminder there was to be no betting, absolutely none at all.

As we sat together enjoying an early picnic supper I began to tell them how well my job was going. Ida asked questions right away of the other ladies in the department as Luke and Jack discussed other uninteresting topics. I was pleased to tell her about the ladies and our fun breaks together. We laughed at some of the funny things that happened while I shared my good fortune at having this good job to go to each day, I couldn't help but say what a nice group of people they were from the stock boy up to the manager.

The Woodward's Family had a reputation for being well chosen. There was a strict dress code that all were expected to adhere to. The men working amongst the customers were to wear a suit with the exception being the Food Floor. There they dressed accordingly.

The female staff were not permitted to wear

pullover sweaters, shear blouses, pants or seam-less stockings. It was said that there was someone walking through the floors each day checking to be sure that the staff's appearance were in tune with the appearance of the store.

The next morning when I arrived at work, I punched the time clock and headed for the drapery department. The other ladies and I were all busy preparing for the first customers to arrive when Anna asked where Brian, the stock boy was. We all looked from one to the other not having an an-swer. The first answer that came was he must be in the stock room. Mildred promptly headed there returning with a slow shake of her head. Thinking he must just have slept in, we all carried on with our duties feeling that he would show up any min-ute. In the meantime we would cover for him, he was one of us. Punctuality was an important part of our duty. My stomach began to quiver as the many thoughts went through my mind. We would not want him to loose his position with the Wood-ward's family. Once lost it was not easy to regain.

It wasn't long before the floor manager came in asking to speak to us just outside the stockroom door for a minute. I wasn't sure if the expression on his face was one of worry or anger. Neither thought was comforting. With his hair slicked down to the top of his head, and slow to smile I was never sure.

All he had to say was that Brian's father had telephoned in to say that he had gone out with his friends the night before and had not yet come home. There would be a relief stock boy filling in until Brian returned. With that he turned and left leaving us to return to our department.

By now there were customers arriving needing assistance to have material and trimmings measured and cut keeping us all busy. While Brian was never far from my mind I tried to focus on what I was doing so as to not make any mistakes cutting or measuring.

Lunch time came with a much needed break for both Mildred and I. As others came to sit with us, we were forced to keep our conversations off Brian but not our hearts and minds. Today the ladies were intrigued with Mildred's new outfit. With my mind on Brian I had not noticed. It was a rose coloured dress and a narrow black belt that made her natural light tan skin and sandy coloured hair seem even more attractive. She always wore her hair short and straight held back with a bobby pin. I felt bad that I had not complimented her earlier. I guess my mind was not all there.

We often spoke of how fortunate we were to get this friendly hard working young man in our department. Some of the other departments felt their stock boy was about as useful as a fifth wheel on a wagon. Just in the way. Not our Brian. He was always willing to help both staff and customers. One day he would be sure to make a great manager.

The end of the day came with no news. That afternoon it was a solemn farewell to each as we headed for the time clock.

When Mildred telephoned me later that evening I felt my heart rate quicken. Perhaps she has some news. But nothing. She just couldn't wait to hear if perhaps by some miracle I had heard something. Usually we could spend a couple cheerful minutes chatting but not that night. There didn't seem to be anything to say.

The next morning a short meeting was again called before the rush of the day began. Thank goodness this was not $1.49 Day.

Brian's father had called again just like he had promised knowing how concerned we all were about our co-worker and young friend that we were all accustomed to fussing over. After both him and the Police speaking with his friends it was determined that a group of young people, both boys and girls, had decided to go to English Bay beach for a midnight party. English Bay was most extensively used for recreational fun. The beach was long with usually a calm water, but with a potential storm approaching the waves were strong and fast. The police promised they would be busy speaking to the remainder of his friends today hoping to shed some light on that last dreadful night.

After another long day with no word we again left with a solemn goodbye, but this time a heavy heart as well. We were very worried. Walking to the bus and then to our home I didn't seem to notice the droplets of cool wet rain falling on my head and coat. A little rain was the least of my thoughts and worries.

Several more days that seemed like several months dragged on by leaving our department with a feeling of dread. We each tried to put on a cheerful face for our customers, but the regulars left us with quizzical looks as though they knew there was something happening that was not good.

Days went by turning into a week, then the next week. There had been no word of anything on the news. The floor manager kept saying that he had not heard anything. I just could not understand how one young man could just disappear without leaving a trace of himself behind.

At long last on a very wet and windy day we were given some closure. A department meeting was called at the end of the day. Brian's parents had written a message to be read to his co-workers. With an extremely heavy heart this task fell upon the department manager.

The story seemed to be that Brian had gone to the beach with some friends later that Sunday evening. Some young people that were on the beach at the time decided to join them. Of course there was beer and vodka involved. The Police assured his parents that Brian had not bought the liquor but did take part in consuming it willingly or just to be part of the group.

After a couple hours of listening to each other tell stories they decided that perhaps it was a good time to go for a swim even though it was now nearing one in the morning. Some of them striped off their clothes while Brian was teased for being too shy to skinny dip. Not being accustomed to alcohol and only a light supper some hours earlier, his judgement was likely even more marred than it would normally have been. With clothes and shoes still on, he swam out to a large log floating in the deep cold water. He had just climbed on it trying to wave to his friends when he lost his balance falling off the slippery log into the deep dark water.

Thinking he was just playing around and would surface somewhere nearby they continued jumping and diving, pushing and shoving each other for a few more minutes before someone started calling Brian. The stronger swimmers began to dive in around the area of the log time and time again while the others called his name. It wasn't long before their calls became one of hysteria.

One fellow that had a car took off in nothing but his soaking wet underwear to summon help. It was a while before he came upon a police car stopped on the side of the road. Barely able to catch enough breath to speak, he told the officer what had happened. After calling for assistance, the officer turned around and headed for the deflated party.

Police divers in their skin tight wet suits were called in. Large spotlights were used to scan the water but there seemed to be no sign of Brian or any of his apparel. Following hours of searching in the dark while the party goers looked on as they answered first one question and then another, the search team continued their gruelling work. Some were asked to go downtown to give a statement while others were told to go home after leaving their names with the officers making promises to not leave town. In their devastated state they made their way home to their families, some sobbing while others appeared to be in a state of total shock carrying their clothes in their hands not having the wherewithal to put them on their shivering bodies.

Chapter Nine

There has been much chatter throughout the store about the new Woodward's store opening in New Westminster. In the heart of the Royal City on March 11th, 1954 at the corner of Sixth Avenue and Sixth Street Mr. Charles Woodward opened the doors to another giant store. It was said that 4000 people entered through the electronic-eye doors on that big day.

New Westminster is a historically important city in the Lower Mainland region of British Columbia. The opening of this giant store with 60,000 square feet of floor covering turned this small city into an instant shopping hub. The large roof-top parkade offered free parking to their customers.

When I was asked to be in charge of setting up the drapery department I was overwhelmed. With promises of a bonus as well as covering my traveling expenses, I could not refuse for which I have been forever grateful.

Before spending my last few days at the downtown store that I had become so comfortable in, I took note of all that I liked and all that I didn't think was the best choice. This was my first experience at showing my ability as a valuable employee and I was going to do it right.

The previous few weeks to the grand opening we spent transforming this empty cold store to one of warmth and comfort for the shoppers that would soon come. Receiving this large inventory of dozens and dozens of bolts of drapery fabric in a variety of weights and colours kept us busy finding just the right way to display each fabric. There were bins of trims, threads and accessories. Scissors by the boxful in three different sizes. Tape measures and boxes upon boxes of needles and stick pins. Even drawers of patterns.

And come they did. We placed baskets of trims and accessories to enhance the counters for last minute must-haves before leaving the till. Little baskets with pin cushions and thimbles were lined with floral squares draping over the edges.

Before I knew it we heard the announcement on the speaker system telling the customers throughout the store that we would be closing in ten minutes, the baskets suddenly were descended upon as though this was their last chance. They would show their friends for years to come what they had purchased the day Woodward's opened. As the lights dimmed it looked as though it was the after math of a December $1.49 Day! Our hard work paid off. It was a success.

As I dragged my body to the bus stop for my return trip, I felt elated. I was proud of the job I had done. I couldn't stop smiling.

Weeks had gone by bringing many compliments on the New Westminster store. There was no doubt it was thriving and would do so for many years to come. How nice it was when a customer visited one of our many departments mentioning how they lived close to the New Westminster store but just had to visit the downtown store. It gave them a feeling of old home. One they savoured from their past. Of course, we loved to hear how they were always able to locate just what they were looking for. The service was suburb, they always added. I thought, yes, that is why we are still employed here, but all the same I felt a satisfaction with a job well done for my pay cheque.

Fritz had a part time job at a service station. He was cleaning cars as well as other odd jobs. One day he said his boss let him move the cars around while staying on the Station lot. It was obvious that he dearly loved his job. I knew it was probably already on his list of what he needed to buy...a car.

This made me nervous. He had no drivers' licence. Fritz was excited beyond measure. He could barely keep his feet on the floor. His smile was bright and wide.

As I cautioned him to be careful, for obvious reasons, he assured me in his teen-age way to stop worrying. There is nothing to worry about. I thought no, of course not. Just an innocent quick accident, a few dents and bruises, an irate customer, an unhappy boss doesn't sound like much to me. I was real proud that he had found himself a job that could lead into a full time job with a reasonably good pay as well as a future in that line of work, possibly a mechanic. He was loving it. He had definitely gained a real fondness for wheels. Once again it was time for another quick prayer that my son would be kept safe.

As for Katrin she had found herself a job as well. When she told me she was going to apply at the F.W. Woolworth store on Fraser Street for employment with the assurance in her voice that said they would immediately hire her, I reminded her that she was only fourteen. The legal hiring age was fifteen. Of course mom was reminded that yes she could. What does mom know.

Well, I guess not everything. The next day I returned from work to see a smiling Katrin standing in the kitchen. She had dinner prepared as was her daily job with a beautiful angel food cake waiting on the counter. I was impressed. Fritz was drooling.

As we sat down to dinner I couldn't wait to ask.

"So Katrin. Did you go to Woolworth's today?"

"Yup."

"Pardon me."

"Yes I did, and I got a job."

"Did you have to fill out an application? What about your age?"

"I did. I had to do some math questions like adding and subtracting in order to give out change to customers. I got them all right too, aaannd I will work in the candy department. I can eat as much candy as I like without paying for it. They have lots of chocolate."

"Aaand, what about your age?"

"Well, he didn't say anything."

The look that passed between her and Fritz told me there was more to the story that they were not going to share with dear old mom, but I could guess. She did a little juggling to come up with fifteen.

That smile returning to her face told me mothers definitely don't know everything. I did know that she was an A student in math. As we ate our supper she told of when she will get paid as well as her other duties when she is not busy with customers. Out of the corner of my eye I could see Fritz just bursting to add something to this conversation, but Katrin had paid no attention to him. She had not noticed or just decided to ignore him. Finally he couldn't hold it any longer.

"Besides being able to eat all the chocolate you want, Katrin I just bet you have noticed the cute stock boy," he said with a mischievous smirk on his face. "He is in one of my classes at school."

This was so unlike them. I think this is the first time I remember either of them parting with any information much less teasing in front of me. Guess they are getting older, and now find this fair game. As long as they are kind I will not say anything. This does bring back memories to my teenage years.

"Well, I see you hanging around the girls at lunch time. So who is the special chickie?"

With a red face Fritz quietly said, "Not Andy."

Now what did that mean I wondered.

Both Jack and I quickly looked at Katrin in time to see her blush. Having had brothers of my own, I decided it was time to change the subject.

"So Katrin. Looks like you baked us a delicious cake for dessert tonight."

"Umm" uttered Fritz as he licked his lips. "I can hardly wait. Can I cut into it now?"

"Sure," I said thinking I had never seen such a

high Angel Food cake. She must have really beaten those egg whites. I wonder how many extra she put in.

As Fritz set a plate in front of each of us we all complimented her on a well done job with no help or guidance. This was her first cake. Having wanted to make something special for her family in celebration made me feel proud.

As we began to enjoy our ample servings, I thought my third bite tasted a bit sharp. What was it? I wondered. I just couldn't put my finger on what was different. Jack looked at me a couple times as he continued to eat. Fritz was clearly enjoying his complimenting Katrin all the while.

While I did not wish to offend her, I felt I had to ask which recipe she used. After bringing me the book, she pointed out the one. Oh oh.

"Katrin. By chance can you show me where you got the baking powder and baking soda from?"

As my heart was sinking Katrin returned with only one container. Now I knew. She had used only baking soda instead of both. The added amount was where the sharp taste was coming from while it gave an extra boost to the rising agent. How could I tell her.

As gently as I could, I explained the mistake showing her which was the other one. As I saw her face fall Fritz stated that it tasted just fine to him. He would be happy to eat the whole cake if no one wanted any.

We all told her how she really must try again although I felt that Jack was not very sincere in his compliments. I would mention that to him later. I showed her where to find a chocolate cake recipe should she want to try that one. Then the conversation switched back to her job. Now I could praise her for finding herself a job.

"So Katrin. When do you start at your new job?"

"This Saturday. It is only the one day because of school."

Somehow the subject then got changed to Brian, the missing stock boy at Woodward's. I know I was eager to share any news both because of the dangers of reckless behaviour as well as knowing that we all cared, I wished to take advantage of each opportunity for discussion.

"No," I said. "Although there was something on the radio news today that the remains of a body had been washed ashore some distance from where Brian went missing. This had happened a couple days ago but was not released by the police until today. Hopefully they will get the autopsy results soon so his parents can rest at ease one way or the other. Neither one will be comforting for them."

A few days later the police released the autopsy results. According to dental records they confirmed the body was that of Brian. Our very own Brian. The handsome charming young man that was so hard working. We were all devastated.

The air in the department was so thick from our heavy hearts and solemn faces it could have been cut with a knife. We each tried to put a smile on our faces for our customers but as word had spread our tears sprang faster. Customers came in offering their condolences to the staff to be passed on to his family. They too felt they had lost a great young friend.

We now had our third replacement stock boy. Perhaps it was good that he had not known Brian. The other two young men felt guilty for taking his job even though we explained over and over that they had no part in the tragedy that had struck Brian. They could replace his job, but never Brian.

The following Wednesday afternoon there was to be a Service of Remembrance. We would all be there. Mr. Woodward had made arrangements at the church where him and his family regularly worshiped.

At a short meeting before we left for home on Monday, Mr. Woodward said how sorry he was that we had lost such a loved co-worker. He expressed to us that he understood how difficult this is for each of us, but was hoping we would attend. We would be seated together in a reserved area receiving a carnation from an usher as we signed the guest book. There would be a time during the service when he would be speaking. That would be the time for us to proceed to the front placing our flower upon his casket one by one to show our respect and love. We each wore our staff name tag.

The service was what I would describe as beautiful, filled with love and fondness. As I kissed my flower before laying it upon his crumpled chest, I was suddenly void of any words to utter my silent good-by. I turned and walked back to my hard wooden pew to give thanks for the moments I shared with this Child of God.

Even though there were a couple hundred visitors there we had received a special request from his parents that we be sure to share a cup of coffee with them before we departed. The coffee tasted bitter, the sweets served were dry, but I remained knowing that it was me not the gourmet luncheon set before us. This would be the last time we would have a coffee break with Brian.

As we said good-by to each other as we left the church, I knew a special bond had formed among us. One that was held together by a charming young man.

This was the first time I had to experience loosing a fellow workmate. There were plenty of customers filling the floors each day, and yet the store seemed hollow. Like something was gone. Little by little it did get easier, but for the next few years someone was always referring to Brian, he did it this way or he did that. Clearly his memory will live on.

Chapter Ten

The end of Spring had come leaving the opening of the New Westminster Woodward's Store just a tired memory. That hectic day still brings smiles to both my face and my heart every time we speak of it during lunch break. We also made a few decorative changes to the downtown store just to spruce it up. We felt it was necessary to make it more appealing to our customers so they too would feel important to us. Periodically we received comments from them expressing their feelings that they had been sure they would be left behind.

While we all worked hard to keep the many bolts of fabric neatly displayed so as to put their best face forward for our customers, I loved going to work each day. To me I was working in a land of fantasy both fun and educating. There never seemed to be a day that I felt as though I knew it all. I knew there was a customer just around the corner that will ask me something that I would not know requiring some thinking with my common sense to figure it out. I loved the challenge. The feeling of self satisfaction that I had been able to solve this problem left me with a feeling of great pride and accomplishment. By now I was forgetting about the little education I had had. I was focusing on my job and the education for my children.

Fritz came home from school one day saying how his friends were talking about the old Steam Clock in the downtown area of Gastown, and could we go and see it. I would need to gain more information from Ida as this was an area I had not heard of. We would be getting together at our place for Pancake Supper in another week so then I shall ask.

If I thought he was excited before it was nothing compared to after Ben filled him in on Gastown itself. I must say this did sound like an area of Vancouver that we should visit. Plans were made.

Due to Luke's work schedule we had to wait for another three weeks to once again enjoy Ida's great tasting pancakes. Waiting in the beautiful spring weather where the sky was bright and clear all day long before it turned darker bringing a dark blue curtain down on us as the night of day set in, we had great hopes of a perfect day ahead. I had learned many years ago that one cannot underestimate Mother Nature.

When the day came it was cool and overcast. According to the weather reports on the radio there was a system coming in. There always seemed to be a system in the forecast. I am still getting used to this city way of forecasting the weather. On the farm we looked out the window when we got up in the morning to see what the day would hold. If it was breezy out we checked the leaves on the trees. If they were turning over a storm was coming. That's all we needed to know, but then there was no other way of knowing anything more even if we had wished for more information. Mother Nature will give us whatever she has in store, not necessarily what we want.

We each put on a jacket and headed for the bus. As we travelled to the downtown area the city life still captured my interest just as much as it did on my first bus ride. People came and went. Sometimes there was a while that the bus was filled, then two stops later everyone disembarked having somewhere else to hurry to. With the number of cars whizzing by I wondered who was left to ride the bus with us.

It always amazed me how some people were so friendly to the bus driver while others very indifferent almost to the point of being rude. Many riders did not have the correct change with them to cover their fare expecting the driver to give them change with a smile. When the bus was full to a standing room only, the driver would sometimes need to ask that an older person be given a seat in order for him to put the bus in motion again. Few thanked the driver for a safe ride upon disembarking, many taking a transfer slip with them.

Finally the bus driver announced that the next stop was Gastown. As we stepped down onto the sidewalk I thought that once again we had just entered another world within this busy city.

The rickety sidewalks had been swept clean with their corn brooms removing the many cigarette butts, candy wrappers and other debris left behind by shoppers and tourists. I am sure there will be just as much left behind at the days end by those walking the streets.

It wasn't long before I could see the Tram News Stand, the Coffee Shop and the lit up sign on the front of the sign next door reading Sweet Caporal Cigarettes I had heard so much about.

As we continued further into the site with the cobblestone streets, I was taken with the unique light fixtures of numerous round white ball like globes hanging from tall sturdy fancy posts on the corner of the busy streets.

The many smaller shops featured unique items to decorate your household from vases, large and small in a variety of shapes and colours to lamp shades and occasional chairs. Others displayed a variety of apparel that had been imported so as to not be duplicated in the popular shops. Then there seemed to be a very busy store featuring flags of all sizes of most every country in the world just for the asking, for a price of course. If they didn't have it, they would do their best to get it. There were books both new and older releases for the reader looking for something uncommon to snuggle down with under a cozy quilt on a windy day with a cup of hot tea. It seems city folk love their tea.

Just as we felt we had walked as far as we should for one day there before us was a well lit up sign in neon red in large fancy letters reading Gastown Cabaret featuring dance hall girls clad in skimpy glittery outfits. At the door was a middle aged man neatly dressed in a dark suit wearing a black Fedora welcoming those interested to come inside to enjoy some song and whiskey.

As we wandered back the streets were getting

busier. There were men sitting on the sidewalks cross-legged with a cigarette hanging from their mouth as they asked the passers-by to give a little money to the tin can in front of them. Others tried to stop people as they staggered towards them frightening them to hurry away without giving them anything. I saw one man wearing an old long dirty brown coat that had become tattered along the bottom edge stopping at the edge of the road to empty his stomach from too much cheap whiskey and not enough food. His hair was long and tangled, his one hand held a cigarette while the other held a half empty whiskey bottle. It seemed the 'night life' was coming out. While it was a wonderful place to be during the day, I had heard not the best as the day began to fade. It is time for us to hurry along our way.

When we boarded the bus I felt myself breath a sigh of relief. I was happy to be safely aboard as we headed for the safety of home. Both Ida and I insisted the three kids sit together on the seat in front of us where we could see them at all times.

All went well for a few stops and then two men that appeared to be in their forties got on. They were of the appearance of men that did some physical training, perhaps football players or wrestlers. I had to tell myself that they were not mobsters. The best way I could describe their behaviour was to say they were rowdy trying to draw attention to themselves. I was not feeling comfortable at all. Perhaps just one too many shots of whiskey, but still we were nervous.

They wore expensive looking suits with black top coats and Fedora hats. Their shoes shone like mirrors. I am sure they were polished with a good wax polish and then buffed with a felt cloth until they had the perfect shine. From what I could see of their hair, it appeared to have been polished with brilliantine to keep it neat and slicked back until it too shone like a mirror. Shinny is better it seems.

A few stops later the seat in front of the kids was emptied. Quickly Luke stepped forward taking that seat while Jack remained in the one behind us sending a clear message there was no more room for anyone else.

The next stop two policemen boarded the bus immediately standing next to them in the isle preventing them from getting out. They spoke for a while about what we did not know as we were not able to hear. I have always told my kids they should not eavesdrop, but this was one time I hoped that Luke had.

It was only a couple stops later that one officer motioned for them to follow them out the back exit. Just as I was breathing a sigh of relief that they would be leaving us, they attempted to push their way passed the officers. Then as they say, it all broke loose.

The bus driver ushered us to the front of the bus motioning for us to remain seated behind his seat. While I did not want to frighten the kids any more than they obviously already were, I just could not remain calm. My knees were shaking, my heart beat loud and fiercely as I knew the colour was draining from my face.

While the two officers were trying to gain control, the culprits were cursing as they fought back hard and wildly. It seemed like the longest time before two more officers entered the bus to render assistance. Just when I don't know, but the one nearest the windows began to lunge at one officer with a broken beer bottle each time taking aim at the officer's face with extreme force while trying to stand in such a small space. Where he was suddenly able to get the bottle from I don't know. It seemed as though it just appeared.

The culprit that already sported a missing tooth turned into a wild man with unbelievable strength. There was now two officers trying to get him on the floor face down without getting kicked themselves. Whenever his mouth came close enough, he tried to spit into their faces.

Watching his eyes turn to fiery, drool running down his chin as more cursing came from his filthy mouth he seemed to have turned into a wild animal. I had never seen anything like it. Two more officers boarded giving more assistance.

To me it still seemed to continue for some time before they were gagged and handcuffed, one to the standing pole. The other to the pole on the opposite side of the isle. One officer was still standing with his boot on the right leg of his prisoner, while the other officer had his knee in his back as they tried to contain him. Somehow control reigned. One by one they were removed from the bus, put into the back of a patrol car before being whisked away.

We received an apology from the bus driver. Why I wasn't sure as it certainly wasn't his doing. It did add more excitement to our day than we wanted. Fritz and Ben both said how that was so cool.

Periodically, Katrin and Fritz would take the bus after school on a Friday to Woodward's downtown where their cousin and I worked. Martha liked to have Katrin visit for the weekend. Katrin enjoyed this special time too. Usually Fritz preferred to be at home where he could see his friends.

Until it came time for the store to close Katrin rode up and down the elevator while Fritz liked to hang out with his older cousin as he did some electrical repairs throughout the store.

Having an older cousin with his own car and spending money was a real treat for Katrin. On the way home they would stop to get an ice cream cone each not leaving much room for supper. I could see Martha pretending to scold her son while she smiled to herself. She loved to spend Saturday walking around the small town with her niece. She said it brought back memories of when her girls were this age. She missed them terribly even though they frequently came home to visit for Sunday family dinners.

Saturday mornings Dieter would sit for a long while at the table enjoying his cup, actually cups, of Postum. This is a powdered caffeine-free hot beverage drink to replace coffee made of roasted wheat, bran and molasses. You either really like it or you don't. I really don't. Katrin loved to sneak a few sips when Dieter thought that Martha would not see. He loved to spoil her.

Dieter was a quieter gentle man. Each day he rode his bicycle to his job at a local farm. His lunch, made by Martha rode along in the wire carrier attached to the handlebars as he pedaled along smiling and waving to everyone that he passed. Everyone knew his name. He too missed his married daughters. Happiness for him was when they all came home for Sunday dinners bringing a favourite dish with them. He thought they were the best cooks, and they were good. They had a good teacher.

Since Katrin would be going to church with Martha, Fritz left church the moment the doors opened to catch up with his friends leaving me on my own. This particular Sunday I took my time speaking to some of the ladies that I had come to know. I enjoyed this time especially since they no longer seemed to be interested in my husband and why I was on my own. We chatted about daily life in the city, nothing personal.

As I began to leisurely walk away I heard Sarah call to me. She always lifted my spirits so easily. I turned around to see her lopping her way towards me with her long strides and usual big smile covering her pretty face. Today her hair had been combed to fall into loose curls nearly to her shoulders. She was such a happy young lady with a natural beauty that she didn't seem to know she possessed giving her an even more appeal. I couldn't help but be more drawn to her than the others.

"Emma," she said half out of breath. "I was looking for you. Do you have time to stop with me at the little coffee shop for a chat?"

"Actually that would be real nice Sarah. Katrin is visiting with my sister and Fritz took off like a jet stream to meet up with his friends so I am in no hurry."

"Good!" she said as she linked her arm through mine with an excited bounce in her step.

"You seem excited about something Sarah. Are you?"

"Yes I am, but I am not going to tell you until we are sitting in a booth. I have not told my parents or siblings yet, but I really want to tell you," as she squeezed my arm a little closer to her.

Oh my I thought. I hope this will not put me between her and her parents. As though she read my mind she said, "Do not worry Emma. I will not get you into any trouble with my mom. I am just not ready to share with her yet because she always thinks she must tell my dad everything and you know how dads are. He still thinks I am seven. You always think that I am already a lady, not just a young girl."

"Yes, I really do Sarah. Dads are just naturally protective of their daughters. One day you will understand."

As we entered the little coffee shop that was ever so small in size but big in hospitality I made a quick scan for familiar faces. None. This little shop was known for their coffee and chocolate cake. There was one empty booth near the back that I could see as soon as we walked in. I had no choice but to be led to it.

Each booth was painted a light grey colour with a light coco coloured arborite top on each table. The chairs were chrome with a variety of coloured backs and seats. Some were a sky blue, some were a mint green while others were a cherry red with each booth seating four of a mixture of colours. With its' well scrubbed to a shine floors in a knotty pine look leaving a welcoming feeling for their guests, it was so inviting that by three o'clock on a Sunday afternoon it was packed with the middle aged crowd. Inside the door lay a mat of a kaleidoscope of colours that everyone automatically wiped their feet on as though their mothers were watching.

As we seated ourselves down Sarah emphatically told me this was her treat. As I patted her hand I tried to express my feelings of gratitude to her for this treat, but also for the privilege of being chosen as her confident. I was feeling very special. I know Katrin would choose my sister Martha.

The moment we sat I said, "Well, Sarah what is the big news?"

As she giggled she held one finger over her lips whispering "Shhhh Emma. After we get our coffee and cake. Remember I am treating you and that's that."

With her giggling and my excitement I felt like a young girl sharing a secret with my friend Mary.

Oh how many secrets we shared. As I thought back to them they didn't seem to be of as much importance as we thought they were, but they were special to us.

When the waitress nodded to us that she would just be another minute I couldn't help but comment on their smart uniforms. The dresses were a Sapphire blue fitted one piece dress to just middle of the knee with sleeves that nearly reached the elbow. The collars were white with a lace edging as was the two inch cuff on the sleeves. Their aprons were just large enough to cover the front of the skirt matching the collars. A small hair piece similar to a nurses cap also matched the aprons. Black low heeled dress shoes completed this impressive uniform for a small neighbourhood restaurant.

As we settled down pulling our chairs closer to the table so as to not be heard by other patrons, our coffee and cake was served. The aroma of freshly brewed coffee smelled delicious. The decadent two layer chocolate cake dripping in melted chocolate frosting with a dollop of whipped cream on top truly did look luscious and smelled twice as good. A couple of sweet juicy cherries with a dark sweet flavour was nestled in close to the thick cream. A dainty fork on a flowered paper serviette rested beside the plate.

As we each tasted our first bite Sarah said, "Emma, do you think this is what chocolate cake will be like in Heaven?"

This made me laugh at her funny questions. It also lightened my nerves a little. I didn't want to ask her to get to her story so I just looked at her and slightly raised my eyebrows saying nothing.

"Well, I have a little something to show you," as she pulled a little box from her purse.

Those little boxes always resembled one thing to any woman. "Is that what I think is in those little boxes?" I asked.

Sarah quickly opened the box slipping the ring on as she held her hand out for me to see she nodded. "It sure is. Isn't it beautiful?"

"It surely is Sarah," I said as I held her hand so I could have a better look at this lovely ring in yellow gold with three large diamonds on top. "Sarah, I don't understand why you are afraid to tell your parents. And who is the lucky young man? I have not heard of their being a special beau in your life. Is there something about him that makes you feel your parents will not approve?"

"Kind of Emma."

"I don't mean to pry or have you feel you need to tell me something you don't want me to know, but I can't help but feel a little apprehensive right now."

"I am not afraid to tell you at all. I know you have made some decisions that were not always considered the right thing for a lady to do so I thought perhaps you would understand. You see I actually met him around a year ago. We just talked to each other once in a while until about six months ago. Then we began to secretly meet. We just walked around or went for a drive in his red Ford Sedan to Brocton Oval. I think that is a great looking car even if it is old. We just sat and talked about our families and our lives. He was so nice willing to listen to me not just talk about himself. I began to feel that he did really care. He assured me that he would not push me to do anything I did not want to do."

Now I am thinking baby? "So what did he tell you about his life?"

"First he explained that his dad works for a trucking business. His mom stays home looking after them and the home. He has two younger sisters and one older brother."

That sounded normal to me. "Did you ask him to tell you about them, like what they are like and what they like to do? Do they go to church?"

"I did. They seem like a quiet family. His parents don't go out much or have many friends. His sisters are the same. His brother Jesse is like Clint."

"So what is that like?" I felt like I was starting to pull teeth.

"Clint said that he wants to settle down. Since he has met me he is trying real hard to live a better life. He has not been in a fight for the past four months."

With that she looked at me as the water began to build up in her eyes. This girl is scared and not of me. What all does she know?

"Who does he fight with and where? Is it his brother?" I asked trying to sound calm as though this was quite ordinary.

"No, it has not been his brother. They don't hang out together. Jesse likes to spend most of his time studying. He wants to be an engineer."

"O.K. So who does he say he has fought with and how often."

"It is with guys from the bar when he stops to have a couple beers in the evening to relax. It is usually over a game of pool or poker. Clint says the guys try to cheat him. They stick together against him because he plays better than they do."

"So why doesn't he just not go there anymore? If he really wants a beer then maybe he should go to another bar or take some home."

"Those are things that I have said too, but he just says he should be able to go to whichever bar he wants."

"You know Sarah, that could be true, but if he really wants to change and stay out of fights he will have to make a choice. Do you know if the Police have had to be called to end any of these fights or if he has had any bad after affects like big cuts and stuff?"

The next few minutes Sarah just looked at her trembling fingers laying on top of the table. I could see her bottom lip begin to quiver. I felt so bad for her but all I could think to do was take her hand in mine and just be there with her giving her time to regain control. As we sat together I silently prayed that she would be given strength and courage to do what is best for herself. She cannot change him. It is something he must do, and only him.

In a barely audible voice she began to tell me the worst as she called it. "I asked him how he got the dents in his forehead. From what did he get the four ragged looking scars on his face, the longest one just below his right eye. He had so many bruises I just had to ask him from what were they inflicted. Why would you not leave before it became this violent?

He brushed my hair away from my face with his gentle fingers as he lifted my chin for me to look into his eyes. I had to force myself to look at him, but I thought I would be able to tell if he is telling me the truth. That was when he said he received them from beatings from his fellow inmates while he was in jail."

"So when was he in jail and for how long? Did you ask him if it was just this one time?"

"I did. This time he was sentenced to one year less a day. The other times were less. If he gets into any more trouble he will need to go back for a much longer time. I want to help him not get into any more trouble because he really is a nice fellow. If those guys wouldn't goad him he wouldn't get into this trouble."

"But Sarah. How long has he been out this time?"

"He said six months."

"Do you believe him?"

"I think so," she said in a voice that did not sound too convincing to me.

"How bad did he hurt the other fellows? Were they hospitalized?"

"Yes they were taken to the hospital but it was their fault. And they weren't hurt that much. I really want to believe him. I am sure he wouldn't lie to me."

"So how long had you been seeing him before he told you this?"

"Six months. He said he had been meaning to tell me but something always came up."

"I am sure it must be hard to tell someone when you have a big problem in your life. How long had he been out of jail when you started seeing him?"

"A week."

"Oh Sarah. Do you really want my advice even though it may not be what you were hoping for?"

"Yes Emma. I know you will be honest with me and you are so good about knowing what is the right thing to do even if you did kind of not tell your husband you were leaving. I know it was because of wanting so much more for Fritz and Katrin that you had to."

"Well then let us start here. Please promise me that you will not marry him, under any condition, within one year from today. Then there are some things you need to explain to him that you must do. You need to start with your parents in order to be true to yourself. You must tell them honestly what all has happened so far and be sure to show them your ring."

"But my dad. He will have a conniption, I just know he will."

"I do think you are right there, but you will just have to ride it out. I think you are too old to be grounded if that means anything comforting to you. You likely will have to do some pussyfooting around for a while until he gets over both his hurt and anger. Then I would suggest you ask both your parents if you could bring Clint over for a little visit. If Clint says he doesn't want to meet your parents then you must say I will need to give your ring back to you for a while. That should shake him up. That is something you need to be prepared to do."

"You know my dad. He will be sure to ask Clint some questions he may not want to share with others."

"Since you are their daughter he needs to understand they have a right to know what kind of man their daughter is planning to live with. They really don't want you to marry someone that won't be kind to you."

"Maybe I will do that next Sunday after dinner."

"No Sarah. Every day you put it off the harder it will be. Also the deeper the hole will be with your father. When are you planning to talk with Clint again?"

"He is going to pick me up about seven tonight to go for a drive. We will just sit and talk for a while. Guess I will tell him about our conversation too."

"Good idea. I really do wish I could wave a magic wand for you but there just isn't an easy way out. Best to get a healthy start on this before you turn in for the night so you can be rested for work tomorrow."

Chapter Eleven

We had taken two trips to the Okanogan to pick and purchase fruit. What great trips they were. Jack drove. We heard that the best and closest orchards were in Princeton. There we could buy from the farmer at a lower price than at the fruit stands. Many of them will let you pick your own.

We did not know one farmer from the other so after driving along the winding Hope-Princeton highway enjoying its stunning scenery we travelled through Manning Park which had been opened and dedicated in November 1950. It is about 85 miles from Hope to Princeton through the beautiful forest of lush trees with the cold clear water of the Fraser River making its way alongside this well travelled highway.

As we neared the outskirts of Princeton on the side of the mountain were five Mountain Goats grazing on the wild grass for us to see. They looked at the traffic going by every few moments just to make sure they were having their picture taken. Some even posed placing their best foot forward. We had to laugh at their ease.

The groves of fruit trees soon came into view, row upon row with luscious fruit waiting to be picked. We had heard that it is best to choose a farm that is not located right on the main road. They would be more welcoming. We just needed to find the right road that would lead us to the right farm.

Soon we saw a dirt track with wild grasses

growing along the edges heading into an orchard with trees laden with peaches. There we found apple trees and apricot trees as well. The larger branches were so heavy they were propped up with long stakes to prevent breakage. Ladders sat beneath some of the trees ready for the pickers. The sign said 'Pick Your Own' which was just what we wanted.

As we looked for the owner we passed pickers that just smiled at us as they kept on picking paying us no mind. As we wove in and out through the trees being careful not to hit a branch we finally saw an older man chewing on a stem of wild grass who looked like he was just the one we needed to talk to.

After giving us directions as to the best part of his orchard to find trees with low hanging branches full of ripe fruit, peaches and apricots, we continued on. While the apricots were at the end of their season, he said there was still plenty of golden firm apricots that we would be able reach without a ladder. He had given us each a quick lesson on the easy way to pick so as to not damage the tree or the fruit. This kind gentleman told us to be sure to eat as many as we wanted fresh off the tree. I could not believe my ears when he told us that. How generous of him. I was shocked at the amount of fruit laying on the ground that to me meant they were going to waste. When I mentioned it, the farmer said he feels it does help some smaller wild life moving through his orchard during the night to find food.

After I cautioned my family that we would be sure to leave this beautiful orchard in the best condition that we found it in, we began to search for the perfect peach that we think will taste the best. Just when we had chosen one, we would see another that looked even better. It was so hard to make a choice, but finally we all settled on the first one we had chosen. As we ate the succulent juice ran down our chins dripping on the ground between our feet. There was no doubt we were now in peach heaven.

With four of us picking, it was no time before we had our apple box filled with hand chosen juicy fruit just in time to see the farmer walking along towards us to see how we were doing. As it was now getting near dusk, he asked where we were staying. Jack and I looked at each other before we explained that we hoped to find a spot, perhaps under a tree someplace, that we could sleep on the ground. As he nodded his head he said to follow him.

After showing us to the area near the back of the peach section we found a shed that held empty fruit boxes. Inside one box lay several tarps that we were able to lay on the ground under a large tree that would protect us for the night. There was also a tap with cold running water from a hose. Most importantly, just a short walk away tucked into the brush was an outhouse. We needed no instructions.

When the light of day began to appear across the sky one by one we opened our eyes to see a bushy long haired brown mutt staring at us. His long ears seemed to be taking everything in. His black rubber looking nose was busy sniffing as though he wanted to check us out. With his tail wagging back and forth, we knew he was friendly. He had the biggest feet I have ever seen on a dog. He must not be fully grown. Fritz slowly walked over to him as he held his hand out ready to be sniffed. With no sign of fear, Fritz scratched him behind his ears making a friend for at least the remainder of our stay.

Again I opened the picnic basket from Nancy taking out some bread and peanut butter sandwiches for our breakfast. Then it was a drink from the hose and off to the apricot tree.

Within a few quick minutes we had all the apricots we wanted, at least for our first trip. It was time to go in search of the manager to pay our debt. We found him on a ladder picking peaches along with his helpers. After a short visit receiving an invitation to return when the apples will be ready for picking, I paid him the dollar I owed for the two boxes of fruit. With little prompting, he encouraged Fritz and Katrin to pick another peach for them to eat in the car as we drove. They could take two extra, one for each Jack and I. As the doors were shutting I said there would be no eating until we stopped beside the road at the nearest pullout.

We only drove a short distance along the main road bordered with wild fox tail grass when I spotted a sign that there were tomatoes for sale. This we must check out. As we carefully wove in and out along a dirt track we followed the cardboard signs tacked to posts as we continued through the maze taking us to a large garden with the sun shining down on the bright red tomatoes. The sign said they were beefsteak tomatoes. They look like they are just what we want. I was not familiar with this brand.

Again it was a search for the person in charge. Seeing us get out of the car, a older man probably in his late sixties wearing a pair of well worn overalls strolled over to us greeting us with a friendly good morning. His hair was white under a worn tan cowboy hat. His weathered face told of many hours toiling in the hot sun.

"We are interested in your tomatoes," I said. "How much are they?"

"They are fifty cents a box. They are beefsteak, the finest kind there is to eat or can. Now mind ya, you will have to pick yer own. My back just ain't what it used to be. They are large and easy to pick. Won't but take ya all a minute. Don't choose the ones that are too ripe. There's a box right over there for ya."

As I thanked him, I gave him my money trying to keep my smile in tact.

"Thanks for coming by. See ya all next time. Make sure the young ones eat a couple before ya leave." With that he turned and was gone fading into the large garden.

In the few years that have passed, I felt that our life in the city was forming. My job was going well. I had received increases to my salary to make ends meet much easier. Our large stucco home had truly become home. We were fortunate to have been blessed with great tenants. We also became friends with them. Fritz and Katrin were now attending the same school walking each way with their friends. I too had made friends that I was comfortable with. Jack had his friends that he had made at his work. We now had our friends together as well. We were becoming a couple.

Katrin was still spending the odd weekend at my sister Martha's place. Martha loved it. Katrin was getting more acquainted with her older cousins that was so good for her. She loved how they doted on her.

It was many weeks since I had seen Sarah at church. Hazel either for that matter. This damp cold Sunday with a light wind, Sarah was in church. As I left the Chapel I saw her waiting for me just outside the door. I headed straight for her stopping only long enough to shake hands with the Pastor as I walked out through the door into the fresh air.

In Sarah fashion, she linked arms with me leading us away from the milling congregation. "I have some good things to tell you," she said. "I will walk with you towards your home."

"Good. I always enjoy your company. What has happened?"

"Well, I did as you suggested. Just like I thought, dad did have a conniption. I would have thought you could have heard him at your home. Clint came along shortly after. Mom had made dad promise to stay calm and talk to him politely. His ranting would prove nothing, she told him."

"Just as Clint promised, he answered each and every question as honestly as he could never trying to hide anything, and there were lots of questions. I did notice that he did not volunteer any more information than what was asked for. Perhaps that was a good thing. Later Clint told me that was because he didn't know what was worrisome to my parents. He didn't wish to bring up anything to cause undue anxiety.

I was wearing the beautiful ring that Clint had given me. My mom told me she thought it was very pretty and that I should wear it. It is what she would have done. Then she told me something that nearly shocked my teeth out of me.

Her dad had reacted the same way when my dad asked him if he could marry his daughter. Apparently he jumped up from his chair storming into my dad's face yelling 'Horsefeathers you will! My daughter will not marry the likes of you!' With that he stormed out of the house. Mom said Grandma just let him storm around for a day or two then she talked some sense into him in Grandma fashion. Just whatever that was Mom won't tell me. She just smiles and changes the subject. Mom had to agree to never bring that subject up again though. She thinks he was ashamed of how he reacted. Mom said that she sees dad reacting the same way. Sure enough, he has slowly begun to come around to his senses.

Clint now comes to the door when he calls on me. He suggested to me that he come five minutes early to spend a few minutes talking to my parents before we rush away. What a great idea that was. Mom thinks he is just the greatest."

"What does your dad think now?"

With that Sarah looked up to the sky as if looking into the heavens to see what her Grandma is saying about all this fuss. "It appears to me that when he speaks to Clint it is not as though he speaks with contempt but rather a kinder caution on his feelings. One day I caught the start of a smile forming on his lips when he witnessed Clint speaking with mom. It's as though he doesn't want to show just how much he is coming around. Actually I think he is starting to like Clint.

Clint has always spoken to me in a most gentlemanly fashion. It is as though that is his natural way as I have been with him when he has spoken to other ladies. Some of the ladies that he knows through his work buddies call him 'Gentleman Clint'."

"Are you talking about a wedding date yet?" I cautiously asked.

"Oh Emma. Don't try to trick me. No. I told my mom that you said I should not think of marrying him before one year has passed. I told that to Clint as well," she said as she laughed looking me in the eye. "Mom said that was wise advise that I should heed."

"And what did Clint have to say to that?"

"He said he really didn't want to wait so long, but if that is the way it is then he will just have to do that. Then he added that maybe that is a good thing. He could show my dad how he has truly changed. I told him that I could not live with him if he fell back to his old ways. When I get married I wish to have children, and it would be my job to not subject them to a violent life. I did not tell him, but I have been thinking that in a few months he should speak with the Pastor for some counselling."

"I didn't know he went to church. Which church is it?"

"Well, he doesn't. But that is a subject that I will be bringing up in the near future. Since I have always gone to church, I know that it is the best for a good family life. You know how we say grace before we eat? Well, he has caught on to it real fast and takes part.

Oh Emma, excuse me for laughing but that little sister of mine, Anna I mean is so honest that sometimes she is embarrassing. One night at the dinner table Mom asked her why she didn't have her eyes closed as we said grace. I could tell that just as she asked she knew she shouldn't have, at least not right then. Anna just plainly said she wanted to see if Clint had his eyes closed. I looked at Clint just as mom said Anna!, but he just tried to hide the smile from his face as he asked her if his eyes were closed. Nope, came her honest reply. With that he thanked Anna for teaching him the correct way to pray at the table. Of course Anna told him he was welcome."

As I laughed along with her I said that I hoped it would go well, and how I will look forward to watching her relationship grow. Then she asked me a question that took my breath away.

"Emma, excuse me for asking but do you ever think of Floyd?"

"Yes, I do Sarah. It is too complicated and personal for me to discuss this with you or anyone else. Please understand. I have enough talking to do with God over this. He is the one that needs to understand and forgive me."

"Gee Emma, I wish I could have your faith. I think you already know that you are my mentor. My mother says you are a strong and independent lady. A brave one too. She said there is no way that she could do all what you have done for your children. I so admire you."

"Thank you Sarah. I am so grateful to have been welcomed into your family. It has been a great help to me to be with someone that isn't judging me for what I feel I must do."

"Well, Emma. I am sure you have lots of people to do that without us taking part."

Chapter Twelve

A few days later as I was leisurely lingering over my steaming cup of coffee in the morning, the telephone rang. Immediately I thought it was likely Ida wanting to chat for a couple minutes knowing that today being Wednesday, my day off, I would have a couple extra minutes. We enjoyed having our coffee together with a telephone conversation every few weeks. It gave us a time to catch up as well as share some small talk.

Settling myself on the hall steps leading upstairs I lightly greeted who I thought was Ida with a familiar hello. Much to my surprise a man's voice returned my hello with "Is that you Emma?"

"Yes, it is," I cautiously answered. Somehow the voice sounded a little familiar but I just couldn't put my finger on just what it was about it or who it was. "Who is calling?" I asked.

"This is Wilhelm. Wilhelm Ziegler from Saskatchewan. How are you?"

Suddenly I began to shake spilling my coffee onto the floor for me to clean up. What could this be about? Slowly in a soft weak voice that was clearly shaking I said, "I am fine thank you."

Dozens of things immediately flew through my mind like a whirl wind as to why Floyd's brother would telephone me each thought ending with Floyd.

"Are you there, Emma?"

"I am here Wilhelm. I just set my coffee cup down on the counter. What brings you to call me?"

I thought I might just as well get to the point after telling a little lie to give myself an added moment. This is the way I had decided I would answer if this call should ever come. Somehow in the back of my mind I knew it would, but just not when.

"Emma, I have something that I must speak to you about. I do hope you have the time to discuss this with me now. This is something that is weighing heavily on our minds. I urge you to give me a few minutes."

Yes, they are coming after me on Floyd's behalf. As I felt weaker by the moment, my mind was making me dizzy with all the thoughts going through. They are after my children.

"So what is it Wilhelm? What is so urgent?"

"It is about our family cemetery."

"Excuse me, Wilhelm. Did you say cemetery?"

"Yes. Why do you ask?"

"Oh. Its just that I couldn't quite hear you for a second. Please go on. I remember it." Another little lie. Thank goodness Wilhelm cannot see me now. I am laying on the stairs too weak from relief to move.

"Well, the town rules concerning cemeteries has changed. We as a family will need to make some changes in order to obtain a new permit. The old permit no longer qualifies."

"Oh dear. That is on your family farm. So what does that have to do with me?" He said that as though I am still part of the family, but I don't really get it. Is this a ploy? How clever of him, I thought.

"We are aware that your parents and your baby girl have been laid to rest there, even though it has been many years ago. We would like you and your sisters to come for a visit so you could each see the options that we feel there are. We really do want your input. Would that be possible?"

"First I will have to speak with each of them. We will need to decide our means of travel and accommodations if we should feel we can go at all. We will need to have some time to think on this."

"That is fair and understandable. If you have a pencil I can leave you my telephone number."

Taking the pen and paper that we kept on the step for our tenants and us to make notes on, I quickly scribbled as he spoke.

"Ok. I have that now. I will be in touch. Thank you Wilhelm for calling."

That evening as I sat near the stove knitting a sweater for Katrin with my mind heavy with thoughts of visiting Saskatchewan the telephone rang. Assuming it was for Katrin I made no effort to move until it rang four times bringing me out of the clouds. How could I forget that she had gone to visit her girlfriend just a couple doors away.

As I stumbled to reach it before the caller hung up, I found my feet tangled in yarn. Dragging this pretty pink skein along I managed to reach it in time. Thank goodness. It was Ursula. She seems to have an uncanny way of knowing what is happening with me.

"Hello Schwester. Wie geht es?"

"I am well. I was just thinking of you. How are

things at your house?"

"Good. Otto has been down with the stomach bug but he is fine now. I did not have time to catch it from him what with him wanting this and then that even the bug couldn't catch me," she laughingly said.

"I am glad to hear that. Not that Otto had the bug, but that you are well," I lightly replied.

"I have been thinking about you lately. Nothing serious just one thing and the other. Mostly how you and the children are getting along. Then yesterday I received a telephone call from Rose. I had been wondering if she has remembered that we are still her sisters what with none of us hearing back from her for so long. She is good. She works much too hard. She says their taxes are going up as well as everything is getting more expensive so she needs to work more hours each day. Poor soul."

"I think of her too feeling so bad that the only work she has been able to find is cleaning houses and doing someone's laundry after supper to help her to make ends meet. It makes me feel thankful that I am able to find work as a clerk in a beautiful store."

"I know lifting bolts of heavy fabric is not easy for you either, but I agree it is much better than farm work. I have been meaning to ask you how your arthritis is. Is it getting any worse?"

"I don't think it is getting worse, but for sure it is no better. I can still manage it. I do fear that one day it will jump right up and get me with a vengeance. Until then I will try not to worry about it. Some days that is hard to do especially after our famous $1.49 Days. It gets so crazy in there. For most of the day we are run off our feet. The doctor tells me I shouldn't be lifting those heavy bolts, but that is where I work and am grateful for it."

After a short conversation of idle chatter regarding our families I told her of my call from Wilhelm asking her what she thought.

"Emma, I know you are very nervous about going back but maybe there is something about this that is calling to you. The safest time for you to return is with us beside you. Have you spoke to Martha yet?"

"No I haven't, but I did think that we could soon take a drive out there to visit one Sunday afternoon. I will try to speak to Karl one day soon at work. Perhaps he can let me know which Sunday afternoon Martha and Dieter will be home."

Just as I said it I began to join Ursula as she was laughing about that statement. "It seems to me they are always home on Sunday afternoons for as long as I know. Martha thinks it has been forever. I don't mean to laugh at them as I know it must be hard for Schwester. I know how much I enjoy going out for a car drive to pick up an ice cream cone just for a change."

"Anyway Ursula, think about it while I talk to Martha. Perhaps you could speak with Rose regarding it too. If we do decide to go, we will need to give careful thought to road conditions. That is not one place I wish to be snowed in. We could have to stay until spring thaw! That would not be happiness for sure."

The next couple weeks were spent back and forth as to how we would travel, where we would stay and of course the weather. Since Rose and I were working out, we would need to make arrangements for holiday time.

By now the weather had changed from a beautiful Indian summer to a cool fall. Now it was looking and feeling like winter was just around the nearest corner. To me that meant that in Saskatchewan it had already turned the corner. Rose said they had already had a skiff of snow. While it had not lasted more than a day there appeared to be threats of more to fall. Their sky was grey bringing dull days filled with a cold breeze. Temperatures were dropping during the dark night. To each of us, this was not a good time to travel. Spring would be better.

A few nights later I decided that I had to grit my teeth and make the call. I owed it to him. I made my decision some years ago and now this is just part of it. I will have to let the chips fall where they may.

A couple weeks later Ida telephoned me one Wednesday morning just as I poured myself a cup of coffee. Just in time for a chat with a good friend. The weather was cooling a little more each week reminding us that it is time to get our fall jackets out. I heard Fritz remind Katrin to wear a jacket for sure today. He is growing up so much. They both are, and becoming more responsible for themselves and each other.

After Ida and I chatted for a couple minutes she said Luke had prompted her to call me today. He thinks we all need a day trip to Lynn Valley again. He promises we won't do near as much walking this time. I just bet we won't.

As we enjoyed our dinner together around our small pine kitchen table that had seen many knives dropped on it, we decided it would be a nice change. My mind needed something different to think of and Fritz and Katrin were eager to go.

Sunday we were off after having prepared a substantial breakfast of eggs and toast. Just as we sat down I remembered that there was a tin of Spam in the cupboard. I did not feel bad that they all immediately said they wanted it cold, just like in their lunch sandwiches. We were so fortunate that Dieter worked at a Chicken Farm giving us the opportunity to buy eggs much cheaper. Straight from the farm is better too, but also a reminder of the North. Now I don't have to go outdoors to gather the eggs or clean up after the chickens. No more chicken plucken for me!

As we rode along on the busy bus to the sound and jerking movements of a large vehicle attempting to maintain a schedule throughout the heavy city traffic with passengers entering and exciting, Ida whispered to me, "Want to talk while we walk today?"

"Sounds good," I replied. I did not know if she was reading my mind or if she needed a shoulder, but either way that's what good friends are for. They help to lighten our burdens.

The first thing we did upon our arrival was go to the Suspension Bridge. It never ceased to amaze me how my heart took a small leap each time we made our trek across this rickety old bridge as it jiggled and swayed with the many unsteady footsteps upon it. The rope like walls to hold on to as we stepped onto the wood plank flooring was barely enough comfort for me. I did not wish to find myself freefalling down the 50 metre canyon to the cold freezing water below as it rushed along up and over the huge rocks in its' path. Fritz and Ben liked to help give it a little extra sway as they walked while Ida and I scolded them to no avail.

Instead of climbing down the bank we took one of the many trails through the park as it snaked along the corridor of towering trees beside us leaving the sun to drop it's warmth below. There too people were coming and going each greeting us with a friendly hello as though we had seen them many times before. Each day I see so many new faces that I would not recognize one from the other much less remember having seen them before.

As we wandered along Ida began to tell me that Harold had visited them requesting they pass a message on to me. My heart immediately fell. Must be Huey again. With my heart pounding for all it was worth I asked, "What was his message?"

"He said he would like to talk with you whenever you could stop by for a lunch break. It is too bad that he doesn't have a telephone where he lives, but do you want him to call you at your home?"

"I don't think that would become a problem.

I wish I could ask him to come one night for supper, but that would be another mouth to feed. Our meals are very basic. He always seemed to carry a more elaborate lunch to work than I can even yet imagine making. We are doing fine. I am not complaining mind you. We have so much more now than we did on the supposed to be rich farm."

"I am glad to hear that. I will suggest to him that his telephone call would be welcome. I will try to think of some way to gently let him know that he must not make it a daily habit."

"Thanks Ida. I will try to do that next Wednesday if at all possible. Jack can take the bus to work so I can use the car. I am sure he won't mind. I am so afraid that things will never truly settle down with Huey. On the other hand, maybe Harold has found true love and wants to tell me all about it." One look at Ida and we both burst out laughing, not to be mean just silly. I would wish him all the best of luck.

The remainder of the walk into the forest was so relaxing. We just sauntered along listening to birds chirping as they flittered from one tree to the other. Squirrels scurried from one moss covered tree to the next in search of something to eat. As people walked by they too kept their conversations low so as to not disturb the peaceful afternoon for others. It seems in the city everyone needs time away from the bustle to relax.

Soon we came to a clearing covered in grass that showed all the signs of being a lush green not too long ago as it now began to turn a dull green with dry brown leaves and needles scattered across the clearing. We found a log that we could all sit on for a short rest. A good time to have our snack.

As we sat chatting about our daily lives Katrin spotted a coyote stealing his way across the meadow before he could be caught. He was a beautiful two toned grey with patches of white and brown in his fur. People stopped and stared. But he quietly trotted back into the forest before they could get their cameras out.

Just as we were about to pack up after finishing our snacks a Cottontail Rabbit hopped into the clearing. With his big round dark eyes and long ears and a wiggly nose, he stopped to check us all out from a safe distance. He was clearly looking for something to eat. They eat bark, twigs, oak seedlings and tree buds. In a moment he forgot all about his fans to return to nibbling on something he had found in the grass. We watched him for a few more minutes until a family came along with their dog scarring him off with his sharp bark.

As we slowly walked back over the moving bridge I stepped on a plank that was not fastened down on one end. With one huge gasp I hung on to the side rope for all I was worth. Just as I did the boys stopped and looked at me. "Oh yes mom, watch for the loose board," he said with that mischievous look in his eyes. Both him and Ben laughed as they tried to politely ask if I was alright. Trying to comfort me, Ben said, "Its nailed down on one end. The board has started to rot that's why the other nail came out."

"Thanks boys," came my shaky reply. With that Ida whispered that we need to say our prayers as we cross this bridge.

With a big smile on his face that shone right through the telephone line, Harold asked me if I could have lunch with him next Wednesday. He had something important to tell me.

As we once again sat in the tiny lunch room he chuckled as he softly said, "Emma, I want to invite you, Fritz and Katrin to my Huey's wedding. Jack is welcome to come too."

"Wedding! Harold, this is so exciting. When did this happen? Who is he going to marry? When is it and where will it be?"

"Hold on Emma," he said laughing. "I know this is kind of sudden. Well, not really. I just haven't been able to talk to you lately. It is alright. I know how busy you are. Huey has kept me busy too."

"Tell you what, Harold. Since you only have a short time for lunch, do you think you could come over to our place this evening so you can tell me everything?"

"I sure can. I would love to do that. You make a cup of coffee for us and I will ask Nola if I can take a couple cinnamon buns home with me today. I know she will say yes. I will bring one for Fritz and Katrin too. Then I can tell you everything. You will need to have the address and time so you can be there. Hazel has two cousins about the same age as Fritz and Katrin so they will have fun together. There will be ice cream, pink for the girls, and soda pop for them all.

Just like he said, at seven fifteen the doorbell rang. I opened our light brown wood door to see Harold standing there under the protection of the balcony from above, looking to me like a stranger that just happened by all dressed up with nowhere to go. I had never seen him wearing anything but his overalls with a large apron covering his plump middle. Tonight he was all spruced up looking like a million bucks wearing a smile that said he was proud and excited as any father could be. He wore a smart pair of dark blue slacks neatly pressed with a sky blue shirt featuring fine white pin stripes. He looked like a new Harold with the same warm smile.

After saying hello, Fritz and Katrin both went out for a while to meet with their friends promising to be back early.

With Jack joining us in the kitchen where the coffee was brewing, I placed the cinnamon buns on a plate in the centre of our freshly scrubbed table so we could all savour the delicious smell of cinnamon. I did not have a table cloth for it yet. One of those items that was not top priority. Placing a small white plate with blue flowers in front of each, I handed each a fork saying we should eat the best buns in town. They are from the Quality Bakery you know. Everyone laughed as I too sat down helping myself.

After we each oohed and aahed as we took sticky bites I poured another cup of hot coffee for each. Sitting back down I looked at Harold waiting for him to say something special.

"The wedding," he began looking like the cat that had just swallowed the canary," will be held in two weeks from this coming Saturday. The service will be in the Presbyterian church just off Kingsway. You know that little one with the tall white steeple that reaches half way to heaven. Well that is the one."

My heart began to churn, but I didn't say anything. I work Saturdays. Just as I felt my heart take a huge thump Harold continued.

"It will be at seven in the evening. Then we will go to the hall in the basement for a light evening lunch. You will just love her mother, Julia and her father Eugene. They are real nice people. I sure hope you can come."

"Yes we can. We would love to be there. How about you Jack? Are you able to come too?"

"I can do that. Besides that sounds like something I would not want to miss."

As I lay in bed with my eyes wide open as though they were afraid to close for fear of missing something a feeling of contentment washed over me. I could see Fritz and Katrin sitting at the table licking their sticky fingers of fresh dough covered in a thin sweet icing making them unforgettable. They will taste them for days just as I will.

I forgot to ask Harold where they plan to live. Oh well. I will visit our house wares department tomorrow. The ladies there will let me know when they have something special on sale that I can afford that would be appropriate for a new bride and groom. I am sure they will be in need of almost everything. For now, I really need to close my tired eyes that are in my whirling head to get some rest. Tomorrow will be a busy day.

After preparing our clothes last night before going to bed, I left Fritz and Katrin with a few instructions as to what I would need their help with in order for us to not be late. They promised they would take care of it all. Now I can sit and relax as the bus carried even more passengers than usual for an early Saturday morning.

I was sure that the day would pass quickly as it usually did on a Saturday. Today's customers would be either those that worked during the week or those that depended on a ride from their husbands or some who required a babysitter for their children. Whichever way, we were never short of customers to end the week.

I try hard to be patient with those that must bring their children with them, but there are times when they can be very trying. Like the young lad that upended a table with bolts of light coloured linen fabrics playing tag with his younger brother. Not only were some of the fabrics dirtied from the floor and so had to be cut off, but one of them could have been injured. All his mother said to him was, "Johnny, you are supposed to be watching your brother not chasing him. Now come here."

Then there was the little girl that played with the rack of trimmings. Some were mixed up on the rack, some were thrown on the floor while others had their packaging opened. A clerk had asked her over and over to not play with the merchandise, but after sticking her tongue out she kept right on. Finally feeling like she just had to do something, the clerk took her by the hand to her mother receiving a, "Oh here you are. Have you been a good girl?" After saying "Yes, mommy," the little darling turned and stuck her tongue out again at the clerk.

As the clerk was busy straightening out the mess, they walked passed her on their way to the escalator the mother commented, "Oh dear. Someone sure made a mess" to which the little charmer said "It wasn't me mommy." Then guess what she did. That was when we needed a jar of hot mustard.

Those are the times that we need to focus on the cute well behaved youngsters that just make your heart melt. Like the young mother that came in with three young girls who patiently stood beside their mother until the youngest one became restless. After asking to have a minute to settle her girls in a quiet corner she removed a book from her purse, settled them on the floor for the oldest daughter to read the story to her sisters she returned to continue with her purchase.

The problems are not all children. Once in a while a husband will come with his wife making it clear to her that five minutes is her time limit. Then they start to roll their eyes, huff and puff, shift from one foot to the other and anything else to silently send the message they are bored. This is not a hardware store they seem to be silently saying. Those are the men that say no thanks to the offered chair we have for waiting customers. They prefer to stand close to be sure she doesn't forget he is there.

These are the occasions in the day's work that seem to stick with us. As I rode the bus home I tried to leave these difficult moments behind to focus on the wedding before us this evening.

Katrin and I had been invited to a wedding shower last Sunday at the home of her Aunt Harriette. This gave me an opportunity to meet the ladies and lady friends in the family. Harold was right. Julia was friendly and kind making me feel welcome and like a special friend of the family. June was there too. June and Katrin were asked to pass the gifts around for all the ladies to see giving them an opportunity to get to know each other in a way that made them both feel special and comfortable.

This happy bride-to-be received so many lovely gifts that at times she was overwhelmed with gratitude. Of course mom and Aunties went all out with towels and sheets. She also received pillow cases, tea towels, pot holders, cups with matching saucers as well as a couple large serving spoons and lifters. I am sure I have forgotten some things that were much needed too. Katrin chose to give her three cookie cutters, her gift that she kept saying was the perfect gift. After listening to Hazel and June, she was beaming with her choice. It was perfect. I had chosen a cookie sheet with a pair of pot holders to go with Katrin's gift. June had chosen a cookie tin with a pretty pattern of pink flowers on the lid stating that was so she would have a place to keep the cookies to which everyone laughed.

The next morning as I rode the familiar bus to downtown Vancouver I kept having the feeling that things were not as simple as it appeared. I know I had not been in touch with Harold for a while. When he stopped by the house for coffee there was so much excitement over the wedding that it totally passed my mind that there was a huge chunk of Huey's life missing. Was this something that they really didn't want discussed or was it accidentally overlooked. Well, I won't ask. If he wants me to know he shall bring it up.

That evening dishes had just been cleared when once again the doorbell sounded. It was the loudest most annoying sound you could imagine, but it could also be heard in the back yard so maybe it was chosen for a reason.

I was shocked to open the door to come face to face with Huey smiling from one ear to the other.

"I am sorry I have come without an invitation, but since I needed to be in the neighbourhood I thought I would stop by to explain some things to you. Hope you don't mind too much."

"Not at all Huey."

As I led him into the small front room I could feel his eyes scanning the walls taking in the few pictures I had purchased from the local Woolworth store. They were not expensive but I did like the frames. One day I hope to replace the pictures with one of Fritz and the other of Katrin.

"Dad thought that you should have had an explanation as to how come all this has happened. He said he had told you that Hazel had passed away but that was all I knew."

"Yes, I remember that. I am pleased to see that she is alive and well. She is a lovely girl. You do not need to explain anything you are not wishing to. That is your business, not mine. However, if you feel comfortable to say anything at all, that is fine with me. I am so pleased that you came by anyway."

"Thank you Emma, but dad and I feel you have been so kind to us we really feel better sharing with you so here goes. I will try to make the long story short, well shorter.

My boss at The Mrs cafe had to come to Vancouver on business. It turns out the business was a family funeral. He decided that while he was here he would visit Frank, my boss here only he didn't know if I was still working there or not. It was just a chance he thought he would take.

When he arrived I had gone out for lunch, one of the few days that I left to have a little alone time for my break. Since I had just stepped out, Mr. Hatcher thought perhaps he could find me. Find me he did. I am not sure who was the happiest, him or I.

As he sat with me on the bus stop bench, he told me how he wanted to open another cafe but needed me to run it for him. He needed a partner. His Mrs. said it needed to be me. I was hard working, honest and trustworthy. When I hesitated he said, "Huey, there is actually another reason why you should take me up on my offer."

"Whatever could that be?" I asked feeling as though I couldn't believe there could be anything else.

"Well, I am glad you are sitting. I don't want this to be too much of a shock for you, but your pretty young lady did not pass away. She has returned and is in good health."

Now I was looking at him with my mouth wide open barely getting enough air to breath thinking he said what?

"You remember them bad headaches she had? Well, she suddenly left for Vancouver to stay with her Aunt Harriette to be able to visit a doctor. He admitted her to hospital where she remained for some time while she underwent numerous tests. The end result is that she still has some mild headaches every once in a while, but can now lead a normal life. No one knows just how the rumour began that she had passed away, but most of all she wants to find you. How about surprising her with a visit? Even just to renew a friendship."

We just sat together for a while, my mind whirling with my pounding heart ready to leap right out of me. I wanted to jump up and start packing a few things. All of a sudden a loud clap of thunder shook me awake. I had not noticed the smoky rolling tube exploding into a dusty grey cloud that was sure to turn into a dark blue sky filled with heavy rain. It will likely be one of those cloud bursts where the rain will descent on us in buckets.

Real soon.

I instantly decided to speak with Frank about taking a couple of my holiday days off. Before I could relate what I was thinking, Mr. Hatcher said that he thought I should go back with him for a couple days. Nothing ventured, nothing gained.

"As they say, the rest is history. The second day I was there she came rushing into my arms throwing her arms around my neck. As I kissed her I told her I loved her. This I wasn't going to say for at least a week. She kept saying 'Oh Huey, I love you too.' So here we are anxious to be married. I will return to operate a cafe with my Mrs. at my side."

"So what is the name of your cafe going to be?"

"What else, The Mrs."

"Huey you look so happy I just know this will work for you. I am happy for you and Hazel. She really is a nice young lady. Good luck to you both."

"Thank you Emma. I have been back in Penticton working on getting the cafe up and running. We gave the cafe a new paint job, scrubbed and washed it inside and out. As soon as Hazel and I return we will have the grand opening. Hazel wanted the wedding to be in Vancouver where she has so many extended family. Her parents will attend too. We will take Sunday to tour around Vancouver for our Honeymoon returning to Penticton on Monday. The cafe will open on Wednesday with celebrations the following Saturday. If you can come, we would love to have you. Fritz, Katrin and Jack of course are invited too."

Again I accepted this special invitation.

Saturday we quickly finished our dinner with Katrin bouncing around in excitement. Fritz tried to be happy too, but I knew it was kind of forced. Katrin told him over and over how nice June is so she was sure her brother would be nice too.

As we entered the church I felt such a calm wash over me. The Chapel was beautiful. At the end of each polished pew of pine was a pretty white fluffy bow with a small silver coloured heart hanging from a dainty white ribbon. The Alter area had two large clear glass vases, one on either side of the Alter, filled with white daises and a variety of types and shades of green branches. A large white ribbon bow accented each.

A handsome young man wearing a dark suit with a white shirt and a pink bow tie showed us to our pew. Before he left my side I tried to explain that I thought we should not be sitting in the second pew. We were not family. He said he was given strict instructions that we were special guests and that is the pew chosen for us. With that said, he smiled at me as he turned away.

Soon Julia was ushered in on the arm of this young man who I later learned was a good friend of Huey's. Hazel wore a blue suit with matching pill box hat. A dainty white daisy corsage was pinned to the left lapel of her suit. A white purse that matched her shoes hung over her arm. In her left hand she carried a fancy white hankie edged in pink just in case a few tears of joy should fall.

A few steps behind Julia walked Harold, father of the groom looking smart in his dark suit, white shirt and a white daisy boutonnière in his lapel. He was beaming from ear to ear. As he walked passed us, he stopped for just a second to say that he was happy to see us there.

Then from the side door at the back of the Alter stepped Huey followed by his Best Man. They looked so handsome in their dark suits with shoes polished to a mirror shine. As he stepped forward he gave me a small wave acknowledging my presence. At that moment I thought he looked like the happiest man on earth. For the first time I noticed how much he looked like his dad.

Now the minister entered wearing a white robe standing one step towards the Alter from Huey carrying an open bible in his hand. Then her Maid of Honour walked down the isle wearing a pretty pink dress over a crinoline of medium fullness. She wore plain white pumps that matched her bouquet of white daisies with dainty white ribbons hanging loosely in loops. Her blond hair was held back with a simple pearl hair clip.

With a nod to the organist, she began to play Here Comes the Bride. At that moment the some forty guests stood to honour this special lady, Huey's bride.

On the arm of her father wearing a dark suit with shinny shoes that matched the sparkle in his eyes, he too wore a white boutonnière.

Hazel was beaming as she smiled at Huey with a look in the sparkle of her eyes that told the story of true love. Her dress of white chiffon was accented with floral appliqués over the shoulders and cap sleeves covering the bodice as it cascaded down the skirt thinning out just below the knees leaving the fullness of the snow white chiffon to fall softly to the floor around her feet.

In her dark brown hair loosely curled, she wore a hairpiece of pearls to match her earrings at the back of her head holding a tea length snow white veil. She was truly a picture of loveliness, so dainty and delicate.

When the minister asked 'Who gives this bride away', with tears in his eyes Eugene said 'Her mother and I'. Before joining Julia he kissed his daughter on her cheek, and then gave her hand to Huey. There was no longer a lady in the Chapel with a dry eye.

Following the short service the guests followed the bride and groom downstairs to where it was decorated with pretty coloured table clothes in a variety of pastel colours each accented with a small bud vase holding a white daisy. A china cup and saucer, a serviette, and a small china plate with a fork and spoon placed beside it sat at each of the eight settings per table.

Soon we were shown to our table where we found a pretty place card with our names identifying us. As it was going to be a few minutes before the pictures had all been taken, June and David invited Fritz and Katrin to join them. They wandered around laughing and talking to each other occasionally glancing back to me to see if they were wanted. As we waited Jack and I were soon accompanied by a few others that had stopped to chat. Mainly idle chatter filled with compliments of the beautiful service.

When Katrin and Fritz returned they were both excited with lots to tell me. First Fritz said he already knew David from his English class at school. While they sat on opposite sides of the room, they knew who the other was. The best news was that David had a dog. He is light brown with black mixed in his short hair. He is part Shepherd with a real friendly wagging tail, and they live close to us.

Katrin said she had not known June because she is one grade behind her. They soon discovered they both loved to read. June wants to take her to the library after school on Monday where they can borrow books for free. It only costs money if you don't return them on time or loose a book she told me. Of course, I agreed June told Katrin that she has read most of the Bobbsey Twin series and just knows that Katrin will like them too. Little did I know this would be the beginning of her great love affair with books. As I too had never been inside a library before I made myself a mental note to check it out this next Wednesday. I had a feeling Katrin would be spending much time there.

I could now see Hazel and Huey returning so we all turned our attention to the head table where we welcomed them with a loud applause, some taping this spoon against their glass. As we all stood, they stopped to kiss while I heard Katrin say Yuck! Fritz just looked at her as he said eww! Fortunately the applause was so loud that I don't think anyone heard.

After we all enjoyed a lovely lunch of delicate sandwiches, pickles and wedding cake Huey asked for everyone's attention. He thanked Hazel's parents for giving him the honour of marrying their daughter promising to take good loving care of her after all, she is now his new love. Everyone was invited to visit them when they have their new home all settled which they hoped would be soon. If not, be sure to visit them at The Mrs.

After the necessary speeches were delivered Huey announced that he wished to introduce someone special. Someone that had touched his life as well as that of his father. He walked over to me asking me to stand. Holding my hand he gently ushered me to the front where he then briefly told our story. When he concluded it by saying that he hoped Hazel will be as strong a lady as Emma, my knees began to get weaker by the second. I wasn't sure I could hold up much longer. Then Hazel walked over to me. They both kissed me on the cheek before leading me back to my chair. The applause was thunderous, at least to my spinning head.

Before leaving Harold thanked me for attending the wedding of his son. He also said over and over how pleased he was that I brought my family with me. As a few tears trickled down his cheek I brushed a soft kiss over the other cheek. "You know Harold, you are a big marshmallow," I whispered into his ear for only him to hear.

That night as I lay in bed rehearsing their beautiful wedding, I realized that this was only the second wedding we had attended. The other was the shindig for Jean and Roy on the farm. Totally different but both totally special. As we walked home I asked Fritz and Katrin what they thought of our evening. All Fritz talked about was the fun time he had with David, and of course the soda pop. Katrin had noticed that Hazel looked like a fairy princess with Huey her prince charming. My how quickly she has learned about the fairy tale stories since coming to the city. They both agreed this was the best wedding they had been to. I had to agree that it was very elegant and charming. Fritz promptly added that perhaps that was because I sort of was fussed over with that mischievous smile all over his face.

Chapter Thirteen

Monday morning I stepped out into the brisk air with grey skies hanging above my head. The wind has already blown my hair into a different hair style which I am sure is not too fashionable. No matter, there are too many things on my mind to worry about my hair after all these years. At least now it is no longer covered in dust which seemed to have seeped through the kerchief I wore on my head. It was not one of a pretty blue with tiny white flowers that I had pined for, but it lasted me for fifteen years. I was grateful for it.

I felt the snow chill in the air a little more each day as winter drew nearer. The leaves have left the trees and lay on the ground in their dried up winter colours waiting for the wind to move them to new resting places. When they left their home on the branches shades of yellow to a rich gold with sprinkles of red and brown had given them a pretty hue sparkling in the sunshine. Well, when it shone. Small children could be seen running around to gather the largest and prettiest ones to take home to show their findings to their parents. Perhaps take some to the teacher.

Even with the cool wind in the air, I thought the weather was a dream while others complained of the wet rain. I often wondered what they would have to say should they need to shovel it by the foot for months on end. The rain comes by itself, and so it leaves.

This brought to mind the fall that my brother and two of Floyd's cousins came to visit. After anxiously waiting for their arrival for months they pulled into our farm yard the last day of September. I was so delighted to see them. What a great time we had. This was the time that I knew my life would one day change. I can still see the feet of snow that had fallen during the night before they planned to leave as we slept. They were going no where that day. We had woken to a clear blue sky with a faint glow of a soft sun to follow later in the day. Their car had to be towed out to the road. That was a memory.

While I rode the bus along the now familiar roadways to downtown I was reminded more than ever how life is different here. In the North, Saturday would not even have been a dream. I had long since quit yearning for things beyond my reach. I thought of the wonderful life I am having, but also am ever mindful of what it cost. Some days I have felt like the price was too high. The alternative would be to take away the future for my children. In my next breath I knew that was something I was not willing to do.

As my arthritis began to bother me a little more with the cold air making my bones feel like they were frozen and were ready to break each time they were moved, I knew my path would become a little harder to travel. A small price to pay. I watched Fritz and Katrin grow into young adults making me more proud each day. It is my reward. Never had I felt that God has spoken to me telling me to go back. Perhaps I just don't wish to hear it the way He said it. Perhaps I have just not been listening.

The weatherman has been forecasting a white winter for Vancouver. A system was coming. While I thought, no please be wrong the children all over the city were jumping up and down eager to see it come. They knew they would have so much fun building snowmen, playing games mostly of snow-ball fights. I have heard that they wish to play boys against the girls. I have already warned Fritz to make his friends aware that boys have a stronger arm so therefore can throw harder. They must not hit the girls in their faces, the same as the rule was at school in the North. I am not so sure the boys here are as respectful. They seem to be rougher and more carefree. They sometimes don't seem to give a toot.

Vancouver, British Columbia has a moderate oceanic climate with dry summer months. So far so good. I am beginning to think there could be a snag to this pattern. And it is coming soon.

We were into December when heavy white flakes began to fall leaving the ground white and slippery. The snow here is heavy as it is filled with moisture. Great for making snowmen. Sometimes when Fritz and Katrin were young they would complain the snow would not stick for them to roll. It was so dry it would squeak beneath our boots. That is not the case here so they tell me.

By the time I returned from work on the first day of the beginning of a white winter land, I understood what the people were meaning. My feet took a couple slides as I manoeuvred my way to catch my bus. From then on I was sure to tread slowly and surely. It would not do my backside or my ego any good should I land on the slippery sidewalk.

This was the year that Vancouver just had to have more snow than they had for so many years past.

Shovels began to fly out the doors of the hardware stores. Warmer jackets, scarves, mitts and boots were big sale items. Children's sleds and skis of all sizes were in high demand. Within days Grouse Mountain became a skiers paradise with trees covered in freezing snow as they glided passed to get to the bottom only to return to the top to do it all over again.

There were smaller slopes for the children and beginners. They were packed with all types of sleds and skies. Apparently anything that would slide was used.

Within days the city had been transformed from a city of lush rich greens to one of sparkling snowy white. A sea of branches were hanging low as they bent over trying to hold the extra weight, some loosing their battle.

The roads soon became a dangerous mess with drivers trying to manage their way home. Some abandoning their vehicles beside the road while they waited for the thaw to come.

The next morning as my bus crept along the white covered road I saw snowmen galore decorating busy parks and yards. Some wore scarves as they munched on bright orange carrots trying their best to see out through two stone eyes. Others had already begun to lean to one side as their bodies started to fail them.

As we passed one yard with a white house and white picket fence there was a adult bicycle still leaning against the fence with only the seat and handlebars sticking out for it's owner to see. It seemed to be saying "please come and get me. I want to go inside. I am cold."

We rode passed a city farmer that had six inches of pristine snow covering his yard hiding the remnants of his summer garden.

As I was riding home there was a car travelling slowly alongside the bus when the bus driver announced to the passengers to check it out. On the roof top of his blue sedan was a white solid block of snow about a foot thick neatly cut leaving the four sides straight and even.

For many people it was a challenge to get to work while they waited for roads to be plowed. Schools were closed for a few days giving everyone an opportunity to search out their mode of travel.

Arrangements had been made with Martha and Dieter that them and their family should come to our place for Christmas dinner. Dieter would supply the turkey given to him from his boss for a job well done this past year. It was his Christmas present to each of his staff. Each of her married daughters would bring a casserole of cooked vegetables. What kind I did not know nor did I care what they brought. I was thankful for their kindness.

December 25th is one of the most festive for Christians. It is the day the birth of Jesus Christ in Bethlehem, Mary's boy child is celebrated all over the world among Christians, and those that are only Christians for the day, but understand and wish to rejoice with us.

It is a time for families to gather together, laugh and eat too much. My nephew brought Halvah for all to share and enjoy. This is a Jewish treat that I remember my father providing for Christmas evening. A time to be thankful for all that we have mostly the company of family and friends. For me this was the first time that I was able to host a family Christmas dinner. We were crowded but happy to just be together.

Along with spring came my firm reminder that I needed to get in touch with my sisters regarding a telephone call that I had promised to make. Wilhelm Ziegler. Martha and I had spoken a little on Christmas Day while sharing a second cup of coffee in the living room while our girls finished the dinner cleaning. Most any time would work for her. Now to be in touch with Ursula and Rose. I knew this was going to involve a couple calls to Wilhelm before all was settled.

As frequently happened in the past, Ursula called me first. She had already spoken with Rose. Ursula told me in her oldest sister way that she would call Wilhelm and get back to the rest of us. I urged her to be sure to ask as to how much snow they still had on the roadways. She agreed and that we should drive my car. Once we got as far as her place she would be able to help me out with driving duties. Ursula and I would be the only two drivers. I assured her that my black and white Ford four door could handle the trip just fine.

After several calls with the passing of several weeks it was decided that we would leave at the end of March. This would work for me. Fritz and Katrin were to be Confirmed in the Lutheran Church in the middle of March. They had both spent two years studying hard for this day. Well, Katrin did anyway at the same time pushing Fritz along with her. I needed to sew a white dress for Katrin as it was customary for the girls to wear white dresses and white shoes while the boys wore a suit and dark shoes. That Fritz had.

When the day came the church was packed with congregational members and families of those being confirmed eager to see their young people make their individual public profession of faith. Their instructions are based on Luther's Small Catechism for those having been baptized in the Lutheran faith. They would now be tested before the congregation. After showing a clear understanding of Baptism and Confirmation they would from that day forward be able to partake in Communion, a Lutheran Sacrament. They have now declared Jesus Christ as their Saviour.

The day was drawing closer and closer. Instead of becoming more confident I became more concerned. I wasn't concerned about being out on the highway with one of my sisters sitting next to me even though it came back to my mind about my second trip to B.C.'s Interior for a one day trip to pick a box of tomatoes. We were all excited for a fun day. Should there be any fruit ready for picking we planned to add that to our purchase.

I was driving along the Hope Princeton Highway just keeping to the speed limit as it is a windy road. I had no more said the road was in such good condition when I heard bang. The wheel pulled hard to one side, the edge of the highway side.

All I could think of was to take my foot off the gas pedal slowly slowing the car down all the while trying to not go over the steep edge of the gravel shoulder. It would take me on the longest and roughest ride of my life until we came to a sudden stop at the bottom in the cold fast moving water.

After safely stopping on the gravel shoulder just before a hair-raising hair-pin turn Jack and I were getting the jack and spare tire out of the trunk when a trucker stopped behind us.

"Howdy folks," he said in a Southern drawl. "Looks to me like you got yourself a flat tire. At least it is only flat on the bottom," he said laughing at his own joke. "That is no problem folks, I shall have you up and running in just a minute," as he turned and walked back to his truck. "Don't you folks touch a thing until I come back," he called.

We looked from one to the other wondering what this was about. A kind stranger is one thing but whatever did he mean. Sure enough, in a quick minute he was walking back with a big jack in his large beefy hand.

"No sense working so hard with a small car jack when I have a bigger and easier one. I carry it with me all the time. It is too small for a truck, but there is often someone like yourselves on the side of the road needing a little help. I am just too happy to oblige."

By now he had our tire off and was putting the spare on. Jack was trying to help when the trucker said to him, "Now don't go getting your clothes dirty. I am already dirty, and besides I am pretty much finished."

For sure he was rather dirty, but with his friendly smile we really had not noticed. He was a big man with an even bigger heart. Again, another moment to be grateful.

As we thanked him over and over he reached into his pocket pulling his wallet out. Taking the pen from his shirt pocket he wrote something on the back of a business card handing it to Jack. "You folks head on over to see Buster here. He will get you fixed up in no time flat." Once again laughing at his own joke he headed for his truck, climbed inside and with a friendly wave he was on his way.

After slowly making our way to the nearest garage we asked for Buster. "I see where you must have had some car trouble. Is that right?"

Thinking he knew this because we were now at a garage what else would we be doing here. "Yes. We did have a blow-out," said Jack. "The trucker that stopped to help us said to come here and ask for Buster. You must be Buster. We are pleased to meet you."

"My name is Homer but for some reason this particular trucker from the South calls me Buster. His name is Pedro. He is a very nice and generous man. Now let me get that tire fixed. Bet he told you how it is only flat on the bottom." With a chuckle he turned and in no time had the tire fixed, on both the top and bottom he said.

"So how much do we owe you?" asked Jack.

"Not a thing. Pedro has it all taken care of. He says helping strangers on the side of the road is he special mission in life. Now you folks have a safe trip," he said as he turned and walked back to where he had already been working.

As we wandered around the orchard that we had become slightly familiar with, we located the farmer we were seeking. As though he knew of our inexperience with fruit, he explained where to find the transparent apple trees that have been ready for picking. He told me how they have a pale yellow skin. They are crisp with a light texture and a juicy flesh. They are normally an early summer apple but there are still lots there just waiting to be picked. If we wanted to pick some they were now half price. How could we say no. They looked so yummy I couldn't wait until we were back on the road to try one.

As we placed our specially chosen apples in the trunk and headed for the field of ripe Beefsteak Tomatoes I thought I saw something moving in the wild grass. I stopped dead in my tracks and waited. All was still and quiet so I began to think it was my imagination. Just as I went to move a field mouse scurried passed my toes making me gasp for breath. It was a grey colour with a long wiggly tail. I did not wish to frighten Katrin any more than she already was of mice, I pretended to be looking over the large rich red tomatoes that lay before us. Now I was wishing I was wearing gum boots up to my knees for fear one would choose to crawl up my pant leg.

When Katrin was six we felt she was old enough to go with her dad to get a load of hay. Floyd would need her to hold the reins while he opened the gate to the farm as he urged the team forward. This meant while they were driving to the barn area she had to ride on top of the hay. There were tiny baby mice sleeping while their mommas had gone off to find food for them. Whenever she stepped on one in her bare feet she would start to cry. She said in great detail how yucky they felt on her bare toes. Thinking she would outgrow it, Floyd continued to take her along. She never did. Each trip was a trip of tears. Now I know how she felt.

These tomatoes are like the round ones, so we were told with fleshier walls and less juice. They are the best kind for sandwiches or just to enjoy with your meal. They are filled with minerals and vitamins. Very healthy he would say.

Every time I walked around a bush to reach the ripest one on the far side I could feel something moving. Eventually I saw it. Perhaps I should say them. They were garter snakes. Yikes! Now this I did not like but was determined to keep this experience to myself for fear of no one helping me pick in the future. As silently as I could muster, I settled my heart to a more or less normal beat doing my share of picking. The last thing we each did was choose a special tomato for the road.

As Jack drove on the way home giving me time to relax and think back on this trip, I sat quietly with my eyes on the beautiful natural scenery as we travelled on the highway that was now becoming a little more familiar. Even though the road was windy and narrow in some places I felt that it was a beautiful road. The clear cold water quickly ran along side at times leaving small water falls as it rushed over the larger rocks in its path. At times the water was hidden behind the clusters of lush trees with wild grasses growing thick along the side of the roadway. Then out of nowhere it would once again appear. The sounds of rushing water put my mind at ease as it tuned the world around us out. There were enough pull out spots along the way for one to stop for a break from their driving or just to let the faster traffic go by.

This trip was extra special. We took the extra time to visit The Mrs in Penticton. With the road being mostly gravel this turned into about an hour drive. Being a stretch of the highway we had not visited before, we eagerly looked forward to this time. We didn't have to check to see if Huey and Hazel would be home. I knew they would be busy working, but I so wanted to see The Mrs as well as them.

As we neared Penticton I had felt so excited. It was like we were going to visit family. This family was a family that had crept into my heart a beat at a time. Fritz did not have anything to comment on just what to expect. When I asked Katrin if she had anything in her mind her answer came back, "Not really." But then I heard a quiet pink ice cream. I knew that it wasn't Fritz. Maybe the day will come when she will have a desire for something fancier. To her this was already a huge new treat.

With a few wrong turns and a couple inquiries we saw the sign in bright red on the front of a well kept white building. I was surprised to see that there was obviously living quarters above. How clever. This already had the signs of a family run business where much thought had been given to being close to home while Huey worked so hard to provide for his new family that he had made known he adored.

Jack suggested that I be the first one through the door to which I was just too happy to do. I didn't want anyone to block my first view, and what a view it was.

As I took my first step inside a waft of bacon and ham cooking got my attention. It was not overpowering nor was there a scent of stale oil coming from the kitchen as so often is in the smaller establishments. It told of a hearty meal being freshly prepared.

The linoleum floor was shinny and clean. There were a few tables occupied by patrons as they chatted with each other enjoying their early lunch. Then I noticed the tables were covered in a red and white checked oilcloth tablecloth giving a clean bright and cheery look. A few pictures of flowers were hung on the walls, but not so many that it appeared cluttered just homey.

An oilcloth tablecloth is a popular thick fabric in the restaurants as it is easy to wipe clean keeping any liquids from seeping through onto the table. Also saves on the laundry, a big must for any family run business.

As I stood there taking it all in I had not noticed Huey standing just a few feet away wearing a huge proud smile on his face for a couple minutes. Then I noticed he wore pinstriped overalls under his large white apron. It wasn't until I walked over to him to share a hug that I noticed he wore a chefs hat making him look even more like his father. I thought I was going to burst with pride. Huey had turned his life into something good.

After hugging me until I thought I would never get another breath he ushered us to a table. "I am not hiding you into a corner, but rather I had always pictured you sitting at this table so as to view the happenings throughout The Mrs," he said. I am sure he knew by my smile how happy that made me.

After excusing himself for a minute, he walked over to where I could see him pull a cord hanging from the ceiling. Then he turned and walked further into the kitchen. As he came back carrying two cups of coffee on a tray with two dishes of ice cream, one vanilla and one pink in walked Hazel.

As she rushed over to welcome us I couldn't

help but notice she was just simply beaming as she said, "We have been waiting for this day. Huey said he knew it would come."

As for the cord, it was connected to their suite upstairs. Each time it was pulled there was a different message being sent with each chime. How clever and convenient for a family operation.

Huey frequently had to excuse himself to tend to customers, but Hazel was just too happy to show off their booming business. When I mentioned that I liked the red and white tablecloths, she patted my hand. "You know Emma, Huey's father had said that one day you mentioned they were the prettiest colours for a restaurant so Huey knew that was what he really wanted. I agreed."

Without placing an order sandwiches were served to our table. The first thing I noticed and tasted was the delicious fresh bread. It was as though it had the special touch of someone I had met some time ago. The filling was of devilled egg topped with a crisp piece of green lettuce, my favourite.

Between Hazel and Huey and patrons I learned that Harold was behind the basics of baking real good bread which made The Mrs famous for a lunch choice. Just like Gaston had done, he made each patron feel as though they were close friends. Hazel also seemed to know most of them by name.

As we stood just inside the door saying our farewells I felt a feeling of pride for my friend Harold. He has a right to be proud of his son. I could only wish them the best of luck for both their family and their work. Followed by promises to return we reluctantly left as we had fruit to pick.

Chapter Fourteen

Before I knew it there were only days left until I would be travelling with my sisters. I was so excited I could hardly contain myself, but at the same time a little apprehensive leaving Katrin and Fritz behind. Jack would be home and Rita offered to spend some time with them each day. I would be back in seven days or thereabouts.

When the day before my leaving came they were both so happy that I wondered just what they had up their sleeves so once again I gave them the talk. Again they both looked at me like they were listening to each word until they began to roll their eyes at each other. Fine! You can fend for yourselves! I thought. Promising me there was nothing to worry about I packed my things and went off to bed for a good night's sleep. This I would need for the long drive. Being my independent self I was ready to succeed with yet one more challenge.

I woke up from a heavy sleep with a start. I began to wipe away the puddles of thick white sleep that had formed in the corners of my eyes before tumbling out of my warm cozy bed. As my bare feet touched the cold morning floor I quickly became aware of what this day held for each of us. Perhaps I shouldn't be leaving them. Then I chided myself for not trusting them. They were now in junior high school with help, if necessary, at hand.

Arriving at Martha's place just in time to see Dieter leaving for work, he wished us good luck and to be sure to enjoy our trip. As promised Martha had a shoe box filled with sandwiches along with a smaller box filled with cookies to munch on. Any kind of cookies were good as far as my sisters and I were concerned. We also carried a couple mason jars filled with cold water for those much needed drinks as the day wore on. We were all aware that too much water meant more necessary stops.

Today would be a long day with very short breaks. As the sky began to get brighter leaving the dark sky behind I felt much more relaxed. Martha kept telling me there was nothing to worry about. Let us especially enjoy this time together. She was right. Our time together was of great importance.

The weather was proving to be the nice day the weatherman had promised. No rain. No wind. I would not have to fight to keep the car on the road. Martha and I held light conversations as we motored along. I could hardly believe it when she said how about we stop for a sandwich. It is very nearly noon. Are you teasing? How could that much time and road have passed. Travelling on a work day had it's advantages. The traffic was light. Soon I spied a pull-out up a head. Just for old times sake, there was a needed out-house hidden amongst the trees. I knew it would have a familiar scent to it. Not one that I have missed, but we could manage it. As we pulled in we shared a few memories of the out-house at home being built by Klaus and Clyde. Such a pair they were, but we loved them dearly. They not only gave us memories, but many laughs.

As we ate we walked around just to get exercise to help us from being sleepy. Fresh air always helps. So far neither of us has felt tired. Too much excitement. We have so many memories from our parents to talk about to even feel sleepy. Our many siblings also contributed many good times.

The scenery was not as exciting as we both thought it might be. The road was nicely paved with no surprise holes. Beside the roadway was just wild grass, some shrubs with a few small towns in the short distance that had there been a need, I am sure we could have found everything we needed. The traffic continued to be light.

We drove well into the late evening before I felt that I needed a long break. I needed some time to close my eyes. We pulled into a small town that looked as though it was threatening to dry up and blow away with the dusty wind.

As we drove around this quaint town looking for a light on someplace, somewhere, we found none. They had shut down for the night taking the sidewalks with them.

It seemed as though we had just closed our eyes when I woke to the sound of a huge dog barking at my window. His front paws were against my window as he sniffed at the slightly opened window taking in my scent. After a couple big gasped I managed to call out to Martha to see if she was awake.

Martha had made herself comfortable in the back seat for our rest. I heard a gasp, then another. In her calm quiet way she said, "I think you should start the car so we can leave before he comes inside with you."

"Good idea. I hope I don't run over him."

Ever so carefully, I started the car slowly moving towards the road we had come in on. As we began to leave this front yard of their neat white home with a white fence needing a little paint surrounding it, I could see lights beginning to glow a warm yellow with faces peeking out from behind the curtain.

While I kept my eye on the road to be sure of not driving into a soft shoulder that would pull us down into a ditch wet with mucky spring water, Martha was watching the dog.

"You know, Emma. He has just run off into the bush. I don't think it was the family dog."

"So who's dog do you think it was?"

"I am pretty sure it wasn't a dog," she said as she began to chuckle.

"Martha! What are you thinking?"

"I am thinking it was a well fed coyote that wanted to be friends with you."

"Martha! You are such a tease." Now I began to relax as I joined her in her little chuckle.

"I am serious Emma. It is the look on your face that makes me laugh."

"Great. You are just lucky I don't have to go to the bathroom or there would have been a problem," I said trying hard to see the funny side.

It was a few nights later that we pulled into the neatly manicured yard where Flossie, Ursula's friend lived with her husband Ludwig on the outskirts of the small town of Watrous. What a welcome sight this was. It would be another 20 minutes to Young, Saskatchewan. That would wait for tomorrow. My sisters were all weary while I was just plain tired. Perhaps it was the added stress thinking of what lay ahead in the next day before we headed back. We four each had been wanting time for the four of us to be together to speak of old times. The good memories and the not so good ones. Each memory was a part of what made us what we are today. We would share freely and without judgement.

During this first leg of our journey we laughed, we cried together, but most of all we listened to each other as we put the pieces together of our lives. Little by little we were unravelling parts of these mysteries while at the same time removing some of the stress accumulated over the years especially by Rose and I for the choices we felt we had to make.

As Flossie and Ludwig hugged each of us they ushered us into their cozy sprawling home that was not so small. Warm and cozy, it was filled to the brim with their kindness. It was as though it consumed the air within.

While Flossie set the coffee on Ursula gave Wilhelm, named after his father, a quick telephone call to set up a time for us to meet in the morning.

Soon the six of us were sitting around their large dinning room table that had been covered with a white cloth embroidered with dozens of tiny flowers and bright green leaves, a gift from her sister. The table was laden with platters of ham, breads, cheeses, devilled eggs, pickles and a bowl of potato salad. As we oohed and aahed while we ate too much of this irresistible spread, Ludwig told of how there was now a young family living in the farm house that Mary had grown up in. He did not know who they were or where they came from but for sure I should check it out.

The morning light shone into our bedroom much too early for me. I just wanted to lay with my eyes closed for at least another four hours. Sitting up late into the night chatting and laughing was well worth the weary bones this morning. The beautiful warm ray of golden sun shinning across the floor brought back memories of our little cabin, but not enough to want to return to that life.

As we turned onto the gravel narrow road that led onto the Ziegler farm, I noticed how the surrounding trees and shrubs had changed but yet were still the same. The little chokecherry tree is still there but having grown tall and bushy showing the first signs of buds turning into branches filled with green leaves was just a large one of what it was when we left. It had promised enough fruit for a dozen families. It has kept its' promise, strong and true.

As I drove closer to the farm house, a friendly dog with black and white hair and floppy ears came bounding to the car to greet us with his tail wagging and his bark gentle. His eyes said he was happy to see someone new.

By the time I was out of the car Wilhelm came down the steps calling to Rover to not jump up. It was too late. He had already given me a sloppy welcome on my cheek while his paws left two large brown spots on my jacket. He was without a doubt a big boy, just wanting to have the back of his neck scratched.

With a few warm words of welcome he suggested we take a little walk around to see how the farm is still the same, and yet somewhat different. We walked over to where the cemetery is situated between the fence and the rye field. Upon first site my heart plummeted taking my breath along. I thought this is disastrous. What could have happened? Then just as quickly I knew. It was called time along with life. The years were showing.

There was no noticeable path to walk as we wandered through what was once a beautiful cemetery that I remembered with wild flowers waving in the breeze scattering their seeds for next year. The markers had been made of wood which have since rotted leaving only a few scattered pieces here and there. It was impossible to tell where each of the graves were. I think there were more weeds than flowers. I know they too are God's flowers that have a beauty of their own, but in their own place.

Wilhelm showed us where he felt the edges of the burial plots lay ending the cemetery proper. After we had each taken a photographic memory picture, we walked to the house where we were welcomed by his Mrs. Opal had coffee brewing. The smell of fresh cinnamon buns was delightful cheering us up. Just what we needed to fill the heavy spot in our hearts.

As we sat around the table Wilhelm explained of the nature of the upkeep over the years as well as for the future. Since it was no longer able to be a usable cemetery he needed our input as to what could be done.

We all agreed with him that it shouldn't be planted as part of his crop. Taking heavy farming equipment over where our family members were laid to rest did not seem like an option to either him or any of us. So now what?

It was much too large to be worked by hand the same as a garden. We all felt it simply could not be plowed over. We understood how it was too much work for Wilhelm to continue alone. This was our family as well as his. Again, we wondered what can be done.

He suggested that if each of our family members wished to come throughout the year to help with the maintenance he was willing to go with that. He then suggested that we speak to our families when we return. As we each silently thought that was not going to happen, what could another back up plan be. I felt we needed to have that in place before we left.

Ursula asked him if it could be planted with grass and then mowed with a hand pushed mower or perhaps a small ride on mower to make it neater for their family and still be respectful to those that have been resting there for many years. This seemed to be a viable solution for everyone.

By now it was noon hour with Opal saying she would make sandwiches. We convinced her that we just could not swallow another bite. We were filled with cinnamon buns, the best ever. We finally agreed to be back for supper as we were leaving in the morning.

Before I could say anything, Wilhelm asked me if I was planning to look for my friend Mary. That took me by surprise.

"Yes. I hoped to but I have no idea just where I might look. Do you happen to know anything of her or her family?"

"All I know is that her parents passed away many years ago just like ours. There is a young family living there now, but I do not know who it is. You should go over there today. Maybe they can tell you a little about the family. It won't do any harm."

"Yes. I think that is what I shall do."

"My sister Louise will be stopping over this afternoon. Your sisters will be happy here, I am sure," said Opal.

After my sisters urging me to go, I thanked Opal and Wilhelm for their kindness and then set out the door. Suddenly I wondered if I remembered correctly which directions. Just as I was about to ask Wilhelm, he said "I will come outside with you to give you a little direction. The gooseberry shrub is no longer there, but there is a different patch in the fence where it used to be. Look for a couple boards to replace the split logs. The driveway will be quickly upon you on the right. I am sure you will find it."

I drove slowly along the dirt road leading to

their farm parking my car under a large Oak tree in the yard. My how that tree has grown in these past years. It is so tall with full bushy branches laden with acorns. It must be happy here having just the right soil to thrive on. I could hear the sound of birds chirping as they sat high into its' branches taking in the warm sunlight.

As I walked towards the door I noticed how the house has taken on a new beauty of its own. There has been an addition to the back, the porch has been extended with a railing along the front. The flooring on the wide porch has been repaired looking better than when it was new. Someone has taken good care of this home.

Now I needed to settle my nervous knees as I moved closer to the door. My breathing was becoming harder due to the pounding of my heart. I must not back out. This may be my only chance to see my friend again, if she is here.

I rapped on the door a couple times with a firm heavy hand. If anyone is home they are sure to hear. It was only a couple of minutes that seemed like many minutes, when I could hear footsteps coming closer with each step. Then the door opened. There before me stood a stout lady to be of my age wearing a print dress covered with an apron. Her hair was a salt and pepper grey neatly put up in a bun at the back of her neck that like mine sported too much skin.

For a few moments we stared at each other in wonder. Am I seeing things? Finally, I softly asked, "Mary, is that you?"

"Yes, it is me. Is that you Emma?" in a voice that began to shake with emotion.

"Yes Mary, or I should say Amitola, I have been looking for you because I have missed you so much."

Before I knew what was happening Mary stepped forward. We were hugging each other as we cried buckets of happy tears. It seemed all I could say was Oh Mary, Oh Mary.

"Emma. Come inside. I shall make us a cup of coffee. I will make tea if you would rather have that. But sit down for a while. I have so wanted to see you but did not know how to find you."

"I am fine with either, but I do prefer coffee. Now don't go to any trouble," I said as I made my way to a comfy kitchen chair that had been painted a pretty sky blue. It seems we both liked the same colours now as we did then.

"There will never be too much trouble for my friend. We have so much to tell each other. Wherever will we begin? And do call me Mary. I have left Amitola behind when Achak passed away and I returned home."

"I am sorry to hear that. I know you loved him very much. Whatever happened?"

As she prepared the coffee she told me of his tragic accident. "He had gone hunting by himself when we were camped up North. He was looking for deer for us to eat. It was early in the morning so I knew he would be gone all day. As he rode through the bush like he always did, he surprised a bear. This was unusual. Achak could hear the sound of a squirrel scampering around. His pony was frightened too. He jumped up sending Achak flying through the air. When he hit the ground his head hit a tree stump. His pony left him laying on the ground as he galloped for the barn while it appeared the bear had taken off in the other direction. But he didn't come right home. Something must have frightened him too much. It was late afternoon when I saw the pony trotting into the yard. No Achak.

Chogan, meaning Blackbird, jumped on his pony racing for the bush before I could say anything. My children came to my side right away. They became very quiet knowing something was wrong.

It was some time before Chogan returned with Achak riding in front of him so he could keep Achak from falling off. Paco, our Medicine Man was waiting outside his teepee. I watched as they carried my Achak inside. I could not go until I was summoned. I must save my tears until it is dark and my children are fast asleep in their beds. This is a private time.

Soon Chief Barefoot asked to see me. He tell me Achak has died. I should now wash his body in preparation for his burial. That evening they danced around his body as they chanted to the Spirits. This is the beginning of the ceremony of delivering the body back to Mother Earth and to commune with the Spirits.

At the grave site prayers are given and songs sung. Before they lowered the casket into the earth

I gave them our marriage blanket to lay Achak on. When the casket was lowered into the earth, the male people filled the grave with earth.

My Achak was gone forever. My children's father was gone forever. I did not know what to do. I sat in my teepee until it was time for the tribe to move again, seldom going outside. Then I knew what I was going to do, but first I had to have permission from Chief Barefoot.

Before we left to move South, I joined with the tribe in their Round Dance. This is the time for my children and I to commune with Achak. We will remember that he is always with us.

That night Chief Barefoot asked to speak to me privately in his teepee. As I knelt before him I felt a new acceptance for me. But what could he want?

He softly spoke to me in Cree first saying how sorry he was for the loss of my husband and father to my children. Then came the question I feared that he would be asking."

"Amitola. What are you going to do now? You may stay with us if you wish, but I feel that is not what is in your heart."

"Chief. I am grateful for the way you have accepted me. I have been praying to the Great Creator and spirit helpers to show me the way. I feel strong in my heart that I must now take our children and return to the home of my parents. They will need someone to help look after them. They too are getting old."

"If that is what the Great Creator wants you to do, you may leave. I will give you a pony and you may take Abe with you. Tomorrow we will leave here. You will travel with us. The next day you and your children will travel alone. You will be there before the sun goes down."

With that I knew I had been dismissed. I returned to my teepee summoning my children to come with me. I explained what tomorrow would bring. We will have two long days of riding so sleep well tonight. Do not worry. The Great Creator will watch over us. Each night before I climbed under my blanket I went to each of them kissing their cheeks as I whispered that I loved them. Rest my dear. That night was no different.

I knew I could trust faithful Abe to take them home safely. Ashenee and Kitchi could ride together. Kiche will ride with me. Soon I fell into a deep sleep waking to the morning light with the sound of birds chirping in the cool air.

It was early but we must get ready to leave. The birds were already up and singing. When I looked over I found Kitchi's bed empty. I peeked outside to be sure he was with the others. There he was preparing Abe to leave. He had already helped get Maovesa ready. Maovesa was a gentle pony the colour of sand. Her tail was the colour of the night. She will from now on be mine. My gift from Chief Barefoot.

I quickly cooked some Bannock for my family. We will take the extra with us in a sack. I reminded them each to fill their water canteens with fresh clean water. Kitchi and Kiche have watered both ponies. I could see Chogan keeping an eye on them.

Then he nodded to the boys as he smiled to me. This meant he thought they had done a good job. They were now young men in a boys' body.

I will always remember the moment when we rode onto my parents farm. The sun was almost down. All was quiet as we tied our ponies to the porch rail. There was a dim light in the kitchen. I thought my mother was sitting by the stove mending the pile of work clothes there always seemed to be.

As I took a deep breath before knocking on the door, it opened. There before me stood my dad. He looked so tired and frail I began to cry tears of love for my dear parents. Thick dark hair that once covered his head was now only thin grey hairs. As he opened his arms for me, he called, "Ma, come here. We have a special visitor. "

Ma still looked the same to me as she always had. She too had lost her dark hair to be replaced with a snow white bundle of curls. Her soft cheeks were still the same rosy colour as before. Like many women her age she had become round shouldered, perhaps from years of bending over hoeing in her large garden. She worked hard both indoors and outside. She was now moving much slower, just like dad.

I knew the Great Creator had led me here for a reason. This is where I now belonged."

I hated to wake up from this sad but beautiful story but Mary had now set a cup of coffee before me. On a pretty flowered serving plate were oatmeal cookies. The kind I remember her mother baking when we were young girls.

"I found Ma's cookie recipes. They are not as tasty as when she baked them but still we all like them. Someone seems to eat them up because they keep disappearing," she said with a big smile.

We had been so busy sharing our past lives with each other that I had not noticed the time fly by. I had promised my sisters I would be back by now. After promising to return later in the evening I made my way back humming the old familiar hymns we sang together so long ago.

It was early afternoon the following day when my sisters and I set out for home. I had promised Mary that I would visit with her this morning for a couple hours. We still had so much to share, but it was as long as we could leave it. My sister Martha had to be home for an important doctor appointment. So we exchanged addresses with promises to keep in touch forever more. We not only needed each other's friendship, we treasured it. It was as though we had never been apart.

As was typical, as soon as the wheels began to turn homeward I was bombarded with questions. Tell us everything, they begged. I was so pleased that they were interested in our friendship. I was just too happy to fill then in on Mary's story. Since I was warned to not leave anything out, I tried my best sometimes bringing tears to the surface.

When I told them how her oldest son Kitchi is now living in Tsawwassen, a suburban community in the south western corner of Delta, British

Columbia they nearly jumped out the window. I too was elated. This meant that whenever Mary comes to visit we will be able to spend at least a little time together. We already were planning to go dress shopping together in the big city just like we had dreamed of many years ago.

Imagine she has been coming here to visit her grandchildren twice a year and I never knew. I told them how Mary already invited me to their place for a visit whenever she comes out. She was so anxious for me to meet her grandchildren. Of course, we both want to meet each others families, and we will.

With having her son Kiche and his wife living on her farm with her, it is not a problem to get away. It was too bad they were not home when I was there.

Ashenee her only daughter lives in Ladner. Since that is not far from Tsawwassen I will get to meet her and her family too. "Is this really true?" I said in a quiet whisper with only me to hear.

The trip home was ever so delightful. My not so new car was filled with love, laughter, tears and stories. It was as though I was riding in one big hug filled with memories of home.

Rose soon asked me how my transition to city life went. Most of all she asked questions as to how I was accepted as a woman choosing to live on my own with two children. She told of the times she was chastised for doing just that. For some reason everyone seems to think my business is theirs and they should run it she said.

"Remember what Mother used to say to us? The whole brood, as she called

all twelve of us, were frequently given spoken reminders that we must not be critical of the decisions others have made lest we need to one day walk in their shoes," said Rose.

We all agreed we well remembered those valuable words. "So what did you say Emma?"

"Well, the most prying man was the children's principal that seemed to have made it his mission to not let me forget that I had done a very terrible thing. He quickly came across to me as one of the men that felt a wife was a man's property to do as told, no questions asked. One day I just had enough. I am not sure if I was madder or upset, but I knew I was ready to collapse. I couldn't take any more. As I took a deep breath I planted my feet firmly on the floor, looked him straight in the eye and said, 'When you are walking barefoot in my shoes you can criticize.' With that I turned and walked out of his office never to return again, and I didn't." He always seemed to lambaste me in front of Fritz and Katrin.

After a few moments I wiped the tears from my eyes as Rose gently rubbed my shoulders. With the encouraging words from my sisters I slowly began to feel better. Even at that difficult moment I did not regret my past decisions. With Rose sharing some of the same rude comments as she remained firm in her decision to not let a man live under the same roof who cannot be faithful to her family, I knew I too had to remain strong for my children. I cannot let them down.

I knew Floyd had always been faithful to his family. His idea of needs were different than mine or those of our children. To me I felt an obligation to make their life better. I did not want them to die on the dry dusty fields as they tried to turn the stones and roots into food. It would be hopeless. On our way home my sisters relayed a few words that Wilhelm had spoken to them while I was visiting Mary. Just that Floyd was doing well, living with his brother but still wants for his children.

Much too soon we were in Regina where Rose would need to leave us. She had a job and three children waiting for her. With tearful hugs we each said our goodbyes to a dear Schwester. We all agreed it was so good to see her again.

I was grateful that Ursula had insisted on driving this leg of the journey. I seemed to feel the stress a little less as we travelled closer to my new life that I now called home. We began to talk of lighter happenings in our life forgetting that we were to discuss the cemetery until we were about thirty minutes from Ursula's home. That was why we were on this trip, we reminded ourselves.

That discussion was brief. We all quickly agreed that in fairness we would discuss it with our families, get back to Ursula promptly where she would telephone Wilhelm that we agreed to go with plan B. With that we all laughed until Martha said it was a good reason to bring us together on this trip. So much has been accomplished even if it had nothing to do with the cemetery. They had walked around picking up rotting pieces of board that were laying here and there while I visited with Mary. So something had been done. We had met Wilhelm and Opal. They truly were a loving and kind couple never once mentioning the change between Floyd and I.

When I drove alone from Martha's home to mine I began to think of all that I had gained these past days. I had lost nothing. While my back was sore, my bones were weary I felt as though I was at peace with myself and my life. Well, pretty much. There was an unsettling feeling in the pit of my stomach that I would need to be ever watchful over. I had once again been blessed, but just what was in the back of the knot?

Chapter Fifteen

Spring had arrived with a vengeance. The skies were a clear blue with no sign of the dark blue grey clouds floating around that everyone dreaded to see. Most days the sun shone it's golden warmth on us during the mid day. The evenings cooled off as the darkness began to fall. It never seems to be a problem sleeping during the hottest days of summer.

It was nearing the end of the school season for Fritz and Katrin. I thought we had best take advantage of a Sunday afternoon to be a tourist in Vancouver once again. There were many areas we had not seen in this big city. I had heard that Queen Elizabeth Park is situated on Little Mountain Reservoir whose summit is about 500 feet covering 130 Acres. A popular meeting place that is well worth the time to visit. I believe we have just the right amount of time for a visit for the price of bus fare.

What a beautiful park, manicured to perfection. The well maintained grass areas were a weed free rich green soft as a carpet. There were small waterfalls situated amongst the healthy shrubs. Some would soon be in bloom while others would be a little later.

There were beds of golden yellow daffodils glistening their richness from the sunshine. Deep purple crocus plants were in full bloom gracing the flower bed edges. Tulips in a variety of colours made eye catching beds in their different patterns to accent the other shrubs as they left a little space behind.

While I couldn't get enough of wandering over the hand built wooden bridges that led to gravel paths under overhanging branches taking us along the most scenic areas of the park, Fritz and Katrin were becoming bored. I suggested that we head for home if they were wanting to go too. I knew what their answer would be before I even asked. They both said that they did like to see it but they were ready to leave. One day I shall come back with an adult friend with the same interest. Still I was happy with the relaxing time we had together.

When we exited the bus I suggested that we go into the Corner Store on 41st Avenue for a Revello Ice Cream Bar on a stick. Now I had their interest. They were so yummy I couldn't blame them. I wanted one too. Today I didn't care if it were to spoil our supper.

My arthritis was quickly becoming more bothersome. Actually it was just painful making my everyday life difficult. By the time I came home from work I found myself in pain to where I just wanted to curl up under a warm quilt and have a good cry, but what good would that do. I seemed to need extra rest. I knew that I would soon need to seek medical help.

Both Fritz and Katrin now had social lives which means having the company of the opposite sex. Fritz had been working at a service station doing anything and everything asked of him. He had saved his money to get himself a car. Cars always seem to attract girls. I set a boundary for his travels which I knew he was not always following. It is amazing what a mother sees and hears. We mothers stick together.

It was apparent that he had no intention of doing homework much less studying. With some miraculous star shining on him he always passed, just.

Katrin had met up with the boy world. They were nice young fellows but one had a car with a noisy muffler which made the neighbour across the street call me each evening to complain. Living at the top of a hill created this few moment problem. She would not give. Katrin agreed to ask him to come in the long way from the top of the hill. That now meant he would need to park on her side of the street while he came to the door to call on her. Another reason to make her evening call. I suspect she just could not be pleased when it came to young people.

Shortly thereafter she met Joe who also had a car but a quiet one. Then the next evening when I came home from work she called me to report what time Katrin had come in. Now she had pushed her limit. After hanging up on her a couple times before she finished speaking her calls ended. So much for living in the city. Neighbours come in a variety just to spice up our life.

I thought it was nearing the time when they would both be making their own way leaving me with a house that was much too large. After talking it over with Jack, we agreed to sell. We had found a smaller basement home in South Vancouver. It also was on the bus line.

As soon as I saw it, I felt that it would be a comfortable home. It was surrounded with a clean white picket fence in a creative fan shape both front and back of the house.

A striking rhododendron bush sat near the fence in the front yard. The realtor said it will bloom in a rich deep fuchsia in late spring. The shiny green leaves against the white fence was a sign of being well cared for.

Further along the fence grew a hydrangea bush with large ball like blossoms in hues of blue.

On the other side of the stairs leading to the front door nestled in the corner from the wind and rain was a bleeding heart bush that showed off delicate hanging branches laden with colourful heart shaped blossoms on arching stems in shades of pink with white that bloomed in spring.

The lawn in the front yard appeared to be weed free and well trimmed.

The back yard was also weed free showing off several flowering shrubs to bloom later in the season. In the corner near the back steps grew a lilac bush in a deep lavender guaranteed to have a savoury scent.

The interior had been freshly painted in a neutral off white. The carpet in a light fluffy beige. Appliances were in good working order but not new.

We agreed we should make the move.

Katrin was finishing her grade eleven and working part time at a Jewellery Store which she loved.

One day I overheard her telling her girlfriend over the telephone about how she was nearly held up on Saturday. Had it not been for the alertness of the butcher from the shop next door who frightened the potential would-be robber away she may have had to do everything her boss had told her to do. Immediately hand over the money, all of it.

Joe was still a permanent fixture in her friend life. At the end of her grade eleven she received an offer from the bank in downtown Vancouver for a summer job. This ended in her leaving school for full permanent employment. She was content and happy there. She had made new friends as well as earning a little more of a wage. $125.00 per month was a good start, and much better than the two dollars a day she received from the Jewellery Store. She continued to work in the Jewellery Store on Saturdays until they found a replacement. When it appeared they were in no hurry to find someone, she gave her final notice thanking them for the excellent training they had given her, but she would need to leave at the end of the month taking with her many fond memories.

I had taken a medical leave for a few months in order to receive treatment at C.A.R.S., Canadian Arthritic Rheumatoid Society. My joints were suffering. While there they treated us with diet. They felt there were foods rich in iron that were beneficial. Raw liver was one. I loved it cooked but I gagged every time I had to eat it raw. We also did some physical things to keep the joints moving. I chose to make a child's chair from wood with us-

ing only hand tools. My time there eventually ended much to my delight. While I was feeling much
better and able to return to work, this disease still
plagued me. I kept being told it was a sign of old
age. It was not unique to me. That did not ease the
daily pain.

The following early spring Katrin received a
sparkly engagement ring from Joe. She was delighted. I too had been young when I knew Floyd
was my love, but still I wondered. I did really like
Joe. Fritz said he really like him. Soon a wedding
was being planned.

I wanted to give her a wedding fit for a Queen.
That thought was short lived. I knew I could only
afford a wedding fit for a Princess. Katrin had always been easily satisfied and practical. I suggested that she decide what she would like so we could
begin to search for sales to cut corners.

First was to find her dream gown. The search
was on. She began to look at some that were very
inexpensive and looked it. That would not do. We
both spread the word to her girl friends and my
lady friends that we were looking for a shop that
carried pretty affordable gowns.

As I sat in the lunch room a couple days later,
one of the ladies said there was a shop that carried
gowns to rent for $15.00. As soon as we could we
were off to check it out. Both of us were sceptical,
but promised ourselves we would check to be sure.

As we were looking through racks of long white
dresses in a great variety of styles the clerk asked
when the big day would be. September 6th came

Katrin's reply.

"Perfect," replied the clerk wearing a bright smile. "By the that time we will have our fall gowns in. They will be brand new, never having been worn. I could telephone you to come in to see them. I will call you right away so you can have first pick. How does that sound dear?"

"That sounds perfect," stated Katrin. "Please don't forget though will you?"

"Not a chance my dear."

We both left feeling happy that she would be able to have as nice a gown as any other bride. No one needed to know that it was a rented gown.

It was nearing the end of Spring when Katrin received the telephone call. She was so excited. We headed over on the first bus. Well, pretty much.

There before us lay three unopened boxes filled with new gowns. As the staff opened them, they held each gown up for her to see setting aside any that interested her. By the time we had seen half of them I suggested that she pick from what she had already seen.

"Oh no. We have to unpack them all so you may as well see all of them. Then you can narrow your choice down," came the Manager's quick response.

"Alright Katrin. Let us keep looking. If you see one that you think is to die for be sure to say so."

When all the boxes had been unpacked, she began to once again try on the ones that had been set aside for her. The third one she tried on really caught her eye. The clerk thought it was the one made for her, but she should have a quick look at the rest. In the end, that was her final choice.

After taking one more careful look at the dress that looked as though it was made for a princess we said our good-byes ready to have our tired bodies return home.

As we rode the bus home I casually asked her if she had anything in mind for a head piece.

"I really would like one that looks like a crown with a fingertip veil descending from it," came her prompt reply. I knew by her promptness that she had already given it much thought. This was important to her.

Since she so willing went with renting a gown I felt the headpiece and veil should be just what she really wants. Again, our friends were put to the task. I really did not think this was something we would find. Once again the search began.

It was not long before one of her girlfriends gave her the name of a store she must check out. Off we went to find the much sought after headpiece was just waiting for her. Not for a second did I think that was possible. And so it went.

When September 7th arrived she had had a lovely wedding fit for a princess. She was happy. I was happy. She was able to enjoy all she wanted within our budget. Life was beautiful. I had been able to give my only daughter a special wedding.

When Fritz and Stacey decided to marry it was in the fall. City weddings are different from the farm. Here the mother of the groom does not have to worry or make decisions with the bride.

Katrin and Joe were a part of the wedding party. Showers were had with beautiful gifts given, and gratefully received. Their special day came. So did a big hurricane. The lower mainland was left without power from early Saturday morning until well into the late evening.

Katrin had to lay on her back in their car with her head hanging in front of the heater to dry her hair. Then back to the hairdresser for a pretty comb out. Stacey and the remainder of the girls too needed to do some imaginative hair drying.

Fritz and his groomsmen arrived wearing wrinkled shirts as did many of the guests. Candles were lit in the church giving a beautiful glow throughout. Again candles were burning in the hall while the end of the evening neared. Not long before it was time to draw a close to their celebration the power came back on. It added another memory to a beautiful day. These are the memories that will never be forgotten. Many brides dream of a candlelight service. Stacey did not, but enjoyed hers anyway.

As my life settled into normalcy, or so I thought, that unsettled feeling in the pit of my stomach resurfaced every now and again. It was just after the Christmas holidays that I came home from work early due to the pain in my back. I was not trying to be extra quiet just my normal self when I walked into the house through the kitchen door just in time to see movement in the bedroom. Thinking someone had broken in I marched straight for the hall to find Jack and one of my lady friends in the bed. My bed. Neither one was wearing a stitch of clothing.

With a voice filled with words I didn't know I even knew, I gave her two minutes to leave my property to never return. I didn't care if she was dressed or not, she was going. When and where she dressed I do not know nor did I care. As she reached for a pile of clothing from the floor she begged me to give her time to at least dress. As she apologized profusely I kept saying get out! Get out!

Just as quickly with much the same vocabulary I gave Jack ten minutes to leave. Anything he didn't take with him would be put in the garbage. Just as I slammed the door behind him I told him I would see him Monday at four in the afternoon at the same law office that signed the papers for the house. Now where did that idea come from? They were lawyers but not sure if they knew anything about settlements. In a flash I made up my mind he would sign his portion of the car over to me as well as half of his portion of the house or else I would go after the two of them personally. Now I had no idea in the slightest what that could be. Guess you could say I was kind of mad.

When Monday came I walked through the door and was promptly ushered into an office. I would not sit. I will not be patronized.

"So," said George. "Since I can see fire shooting from your eyes I would say there is a problem concerning Jack. Now that is just a guess. Am I correct?"

"Yes. I apologize if I seem rude but it is not you I have an issue with. Here is what I want, or rather need from someone here."

After an explanation as to what had taken place he calmly said he knew his wife would have done the same thing except he likely would be wearing a lampshade. With that I had to smile a little, just a little.

As soon as I was joined with his co-worker Ian, George and I filled him in. I explained what I expected. Before anything more could be done Jack needed to be called in. Their secretary then read him the short version of what I had said and expected. Much to my surprise he agreed and was ready to sign the necessary papers if for no other reason than to get out the door.

Just as he was about to go through the door Ian said, "Oh Jack. There is one more thing. You need to pay for half of this visit."

As I held my breath waiting for him to object he took out his wallet handing some paper money to Ian, turned and left. He was now out of my life. How could I have been so stupid.

I spent the remainder of the evening and night beating myself up for following such a dumb path. I should have known better. For this I had no one to blame but myself. About four in the morning I decided it was time to pick myself up by my bootstraps and get on with it. This was getting me nowhere and I soon needed to be at work.

It took a while before I felt I was able to get on with life. The mistrust hurt me as much as his disrespect for me. My lady friends were very generous with their time sharing much of it with me either in person or with telephone calls. Before I knew it my life was now on a smooth path where I could handle it without someone there to pick me up at the end of the day. I had chosen to pour my heart into my job to keep my mind from overreacting any more than it already had. I still felt mad at myself for being so naive to be used in such a way. Apparently his little affair had been going on for a while according to my neighbour. That made me feel even dumber.

Some months later I picked up a full bolt of a heavier fabric to move it to another more attractive table when I felt a pinch in my back. It felt as though something had cracked. The next day was Wednesday. Thank goodness. I would see the doctor in the afternoon, but first I knew I would be having to deal with some pain as well as a sleepless night.

Following a thorough examination he insisted that I have some x-rays taken. I should see him again the following Wednesday after I finished working at noon. With some pain pills and walking very gingerly I managed to get through another week. My co-workers were very good to me helping me out at every turn. I could not afford to take a week off work with no pay.

A week later I received the unhappy news. I needed to take an early retirement due to the nerve root compression related to a lumbar disc protrusion. Along with the arthritis that was already invading my major joints it was imperative to take this early retirement right away. He would sign the necessary papers for medical leave with compensation benefits.

Joe had already been suggesting that I sell the house to move into something like their older friends were living in. A single wide mobile home in South Surrey. Perhaps the time has come.

Sunday after lunch it was time to pay them a visit. I had always known that God works in mysterious ways. As I drove through the complex to their home I passed a well taken care of single wide for sale. It was now or never. I walked up to the door with no appointment. They offered to show their home to me. I was interested.

Following a short visit I returned home to contact a realtor. They worked hard to help me sell my home so I could purchase a smaller home in a more relaxed atmosphere as quickly as possible. I soon fell into a new life loving my own home more each day. Without outwardly saying so I knew my children were happy to see me move to something smaller without the upkeep that I could no longer do by myself.

I soon joined the Senior Centre where I made numerous friends quickly becoming involved in new activities that kept both my mind and body active. The times that I felt just too bad to go, I could stay home or I could go and just enjoy their company. I played cards, mostly whist and euchre that I was familiar with. I carpet bowled once a week in the afternoon. I sang with the Sweet Adelines, a group of sixteen ladies with a great director, that extends over five continents proudly wearing my long flowered dress in blue identifying me as a member of this sought after position. First thing I did was let the members know that I did not know how to read music. It upset no one. We entertained the shut-ins as well as other local groups. I enjoyed meeting so many new people. My circle of friends was getting larger much to my delight.

I became an active member of the Senior Centre that worked hard to raise funds to keep the Centre operating. It needed a cabinet to display handcraft items members had made for sale, but it cost money. I approached the City Council for their help to no avail, but I would not give up. Finally I felt like I was giving something back to the community.

Just as I was beginning to relax into a routine I was asked to join a four people senior band. The Orchids. They needed a replacement on the drums. The first thing I did was explain that I did not know how to read music and I have never touched a drum in my entire life. My ear for music was fair and my rhythm was good. Once more I was assured this was not a problem. The rest they would teach me. It was so much fun I could not believe it took me so many years to try this new adventure. At last life was more fun than work.

Joe had insisted that he build an add-on room to my home. It was small keeping with the city By-laws, but would make room for a few extra things as well as a small table should I decide to get interested in ceramics. Now when did he think I would have time for that. Well, it didn't take long. I loved it. It was also supposed to be good for keeping my hands and fingers moving. There was only so much that I could use so I made items for my family, everything from soap dishes to wall hangers and cake plates. With the small electric heater I could putter well into the evening. One evening I realized that I was now back enjoying singing my favourite hymns if only to myself. My work room was soon filled with familiar hymns from long ago.

A year later we had saved enough money to purchase a cabinet with a lock and key for our handcrafts at the Senior Centre. From now on the only items leaving would be the ones that were paid for. Our reward for a hard job well done.

A big excitement in my life was now having grandchildren. First came Dawn, then Hunter, Gina and Bruce. Dawn and Bruce were Katrin's. Hunter and Gina were Fritz's. How blessed could I be to have two granddaughters and two grandsons, all healthy and full of life. Now I understood what my friends meant when they would say "just wait until you have grandchildren. They are soooo cute." They were right. Mine were smart too. $1.49 Day was just the perfect day to shop for young children. Imagine a sweater for a $1.49.

I was so preoccupied with my busy life that I had forgotten about my friends at Quality Bakery until one day I bumped into Nola in the supermarket. After our surprise at seeing the other, Nola said they were wondering how to locate me. The neighbours from my house in South Vancouver said they had no forwarding address.

"Never mind that now," said Nola. "I have

found you in time to invite you to our reunion. It is in two weeks on a Sunday afternoon. It is in the basement of Harold's church. Well, you know the one Huey was married in. Can you come?"

"Of course I can. I would love to see everyone again. What can I bring?"

"Not a thing. Frank and I have it covered. It will not be fancy but we will have a fun time just getting caught up on each other's lives." With that she turned waving a friendly good bye as she hurried down the street.

I couldn't help but wonder what brought this party on. Must be something important after all these years. Nevertheless, it will be fun.

Now I began to think of my friend Mary. I wonder if she has tried to contact me or has she just not been out here visiting with Ashenee. When I get home I must look up a telephone number so I don't loose touch again.

Later that evening when I felt that they will have finished their supper I dialled Ashenee's number. After a couple rings I heard the voice of a young child. This must be Mary's grandchild.

Mary had just arrived the day before for a visit. She would be here for a couple weeks.

"Emma, I have been missing you so much. Can we spend the day together real soon?"

"We sure can Mary. I am too excited to wait much longer. How about we take the bus to the Park Royal Shopping Centre in North Vancouver. We may just as well make a day of it if that is alright with you."

"That will be perfect. I have never been there. Now let me see. That is how many sleeps?"

As I went about my social life the next few days chuckling over our counting sleeps as we did as young girls, the time passed quickly. As I walked to the bus stop where we would meet I reminded myself to enjoy the beauty around me. The sky was clear with very little of city smog to spoil the view. It was just cool enough that I needed to wear a summer coat. This was a special day so we agreed to dress up a little just like we had said we would, but we never got to. Today we were going to make it special and fun.

The bus ride was long but passed quickly as we both enjoyed the scenery of a large city passing us by. We easily filled in the time with some reminiscing interlaced with sharing our current pieces of life. At times we were laughing and the next minute we were sharing tears of our sadder times. While it was difficult to do I explained a shortened version of my years spent with Jack, the beginning and the end. There was no judgment but isn't that how true friends respond. She agreed with me that the most important thing was to make my piece with God and then move on. We each need to remember it is not our job to judge, God will take care of that in His time and way.

As we entered the Woodward's Store that held the same appearance as the downtown store only a smaller version, our mood lightened up. We were here to have fun. The first department that Mary wanted to visit was the drapery department. There were only a few clerks that I had met before surprising me with a warm and friendly hello. When we left that department we headed to the ladies' wear, the fun department.

The first area was the spring and summer coats. What fun we had admiring the many colours and styles in a variety of lengths. With one quick look at each other we just knew we were meant to model coats. What fun we had trying them on as we strutted down the aisles not caring if there was anyone there to see or not. We were in a world all our own as we portrayed that of a model, a very inexperienced one.

Next we found the hats in many spring colours and styles. Some were just right for us while others we could not imagine who would wish to wear them especially the ones with the matching open fan standing along the top with large full bows to match along both sides. They were for sure meant for a class above us. We did see a couple fancy cowgirl hats with tulle and feathers in the back matching the colour of the velour. We both agreed we would have loved them in our farm days. We both agreed that the pill box hats of today were more reasonable for the middle class lady. Mine had a matching veil that covered the forehead in blue.

"That sounds like mine except mine is a light brown colour," said Mary.

As much as we admired the new fashions neither of us had a desire to get serious about making a purchase. There just was not a must have item, at least not in our price range.

We took our time enjoying our lunch in a small cafe situated near the middle of the mall. There were no table cloths but there were comfortable chairs and clean bright tables. Tall glasses of cold water was served as we sat down. The menu was only one page of delicious sounding sandwiches. They sounded so good we had a hard time to decide. Just the thought of not having to make it ourselves was a treat in itself. Salmon it was for both of us with a cup of hot coffee. The desert of the day was either a slice of pie or a slice of chocolate cake. Mary chose banana cream pie while I chose the cake. It was delicious but not nearly as fancy as the layered cake Sarah had treated me to. Today the company was a little more special.

As we rode the bus home Mary suggested that before she returns to the farm we go out for coffee one afternoon taking Dawn and Ashenee with us. What a great idea. I just knew Dawn would love to see Ashenee again. Then I suggested that we go to Rose's Tea House in South Surrey. It is a quaint small building that looks like something from a fairy tale book on the outside painted in an array of soft pastel colours. The tables are round with dainty table cloths and matching serviettes. They use real china tea cups with saucers for each. My list could go on but I think you should wait to see the remainder of the inside first hand I had said. It is almost too much to absorb.

"Mary, I do not wish to upset you, but have been wondering how you are managing to change back into a different life, one without Achak and his ways," I asked.

"It was a little hard at first. I had gotten so used to speaking another language as did my children. I had tried to teach them a little English but a few words later Cree would pop out. Now we all are proud to be in our new life. I know it is what Achak would have wanted for us. Of course some customs are different, but when you have young ones in school it soon becomes a natural part of one's life.

I am not sorry that I left with Achak but am grateful that I was able to return to my people when I did. I had missed my parents and home so much, but it was the right thing to do. My mother said she told you about my natural father. That explained a lot of my questions and feeling toward them."

The two weeks had passed quickly and before I knew it I was off to the church to meet the group from Quality Bakery for an afternoon of social time. As I entered through the white door I felt both excitement and nervousness. They did not know of the changes in my life. There were very few friends that I told the complete story to. The remainder I just said that we decided to go our separate ways. If they wished to think there was more to it than that, it was fine with me. I have become fairly good at changing the subject rather quickly. Likely I shall have more practice today.

The first person to greet me as I entered the Parish Hall was Nola just as I should have expected. She was the hostess, and such a beautiful one she was. She was dressed in an apple green dress that barely covered her knees. The A-line design of the skirt gave the added fullness of elegance. The rich pearls that hung loosely around her neck added to her beauty bringing out the natural colour of her complexion. Her pearl earrings were a plain large button style to match the necklace.

Nola immediately linked her arm through mine as she led me into the crowd gathered in the centre of the room announcing loudly for all to hear, "Does everyone here remember Emma. She is the one that can bake great bread because she can knead that dough until it squeaks in no time. Now I don't mean that our other bread bakers are not doing a good job. Oh dear. I surely didn't explain that just right, did I?"

That turned out to be an ice breaker. Everyone laughed with a few funny comments being returned that Nola took in good stride. Seems there was no hard feelings in that room.

After Nola had announced a couple times that she wished everyone would visit the food table helping themselves to anything they wished I thought I would do just that. There was tea, coffee and juice on the smaller square table in the corner. There were no reserved tables so just make yourself comfortable she had said. Frank announced in his usual manner that all compliments could come his way after all he did all the baking. With that the kidding began in earnest. Nola had told us how he couldn't make himself a slice of toast without burning it.

Harold motioned for me to join him and another lady that he promptly introduced to me as Shirley, a new lady to the staff. After a few minutes of idle chatter I just had to ask him how Huey is doing.

"Huey and Hazel are doing just fine. They have a little banbino already with another on the way. They don't care if it should be a bambino or a bambina, just wishing for a happy and healthy baby."

"That is so good. I am happy for them. I don't even need to ask how you like being a grandpa. Do you have him spoiled yet?"

"As much as I would kind of like to spoil him, Hazel has warned me to shower him with love and attention, but she does not want a brat to raise. She is pretty firm so he will grow up to be a fine young man I am sure. She stands her own beside my Huey too," he said as he laughed. "She has been so good for him. My Huey just adores her, and doesn't mind showing it."

"So what is happening with The Mrs?"

"It is growing real nice. Gaston has always been ready to help teach him all the things they needed to learn about a business. Hazel has learned to do the books from Julia. She is a real smart young lady. She calls me her daddy just like Eugene. I sure had to wait a long time to get a daughter but now I have the best. I love her as much as my Huey."

I told Harold how I had received a Christmas card from Julia and Eugene inviting me to visit them for a couple days this summer. Now for sure I will try to arrange a time when it will suit them for a short visit. I wondered if the little bambino looks like his daddy or his mommy. Not that it matters. How can a baby not be cute I asked myself.

As I noticed people beginning to leave, I said to Harold and Shirley that I would say goodbye to Nola and Frank and then be on my way. Shirley said goodbye to both of us saying she was going to visit the ladies' room and then head for home.

When she had moved out of hearing Harold asked me where Jack was. In a brief rendition of my story, I explained what had happened.

"I am so sorry to hear that Emma. That is unfortunate but do not blame yourself. He did what he wished to do regardless of your feelings or his commitment to your relationship. You can move on. If I should bump into him I shall tell him so."

"Thanks Harold but it is quite alright. I am busy and happy with my life as it is. I know now that I have what is really important to me."

Later that evening as I sat in my comfy chair watching a Lawrence Welk Show with his big band as they played their favourite songs of the 70's I felt so content thinking of the warm and friendly time I had been able to enjoy earlier in the afternoon. Norma Zimmer, my favourite member of his cast is just about to sing again. I could listen to her for hours on end. She has such a sweet delicate voice and beautiful hair. At that thought I had to smile.

A couple days later I walked over to the Amenity Hall in our complex complete with a fireplace, a pool table, a card table holding a puzzle in the process of being completed with soft sitting chairs at the four tables where many sat to chat with a neighbour or a friend. This is where the Sweet Adelines practice using the mahogany piano that sported a little dust most days. A Men's Choir group of nine strong voices singing Harmony, mostly husbands performing for our audiences as well for added entertainment. Because our area is not large enough to warrant two separate choirs, we each sing a couple numbers before joining together for a closing song. We are so thankful for a director with the talent to put it all together making us a popular Mixed Choir eager to perform for others.

Just as we were doing a run through to make sure we had it all together for our next performance one of the men fell to the floor. Those around him thought that he had fainted from standing too long. Not sure if it was the shock to us that one of the healthiest of our own had fallen, it seemed that life stood still for a moment.

There not being a telephone in the hall, one of the men set out on foot in search of someone home that lived nearby. I know it was not long before he returned, but it seemed like a very long time. The ambulance was on it's way. I found myself saying breath Peter, breath Peter as though it would help him.

Soon Peter was on his way to the Peace Arch Hospital under the expert care of the ambulance attendants. Before departing for the night his friend Henry said he would keep us informed. He would call four people who said they in turn would each call a couple others. Peter was breathing but on oxygen when they left, but it still gave each of us a sleepless night. The next day we each received word that they were doing precautionary testing so therefore he would be staying for a couple more days just to be sure. That was good news.

I knew I would not go directly to sleep when I returned, so after a hot shower I made myself a cup of weak tea to sip on while I spent a little time crocheting a doily I had been working on for some time. This kept my hands busy but my mind was free to reminisce.

For some reason Bruce came to my mind. Since he got his drivers license he has been so good to pick me up when the weather is dark and wet. He has also been doing extra tough chores for me. Many a time he comes to mow my lawn. Then we sit and enjoy a bottle of cream soda and some cookies as we chat. He always seems to leave me with something funny to think about. Tonight it came to my mind of the last time he came to clean the gutters for me. It still makes me laugh. I am not sure anymore just what happened but somehow I got pretty wet.

Then my mind went back to the many times Joe and Katrin picked me up on a Sunday afternoon to go to Ferndale, Washington for a drive stopping in at their favourite fish and chip place when they were not in the vicinity of Moby Dick's. It was just a nice drive. I always sat in the middle in the back seat with Dawn snuggled up to me on my left side while Bruce snuggled in on my right side. In the winter months I was sure to wear my brown faux fur jacket as they both loved to sit close running their fingers along the soft feel of the sleeves.

Skippers was a popular small restaurant, fast food style that was known for serving halibut and chips that were always cooked to perfection. They were never greasy, and always served with an ample amount of tarter sauce. The portions served in red plastic oval baskets were generous. They were so large that we never ordered a basket for Bruce. Instead he got to choose his favourite item from each basket including the deep fried prawns we added to each order.

On the ride home we all helped ourselves to cookies from my cookie tin. Then it was time for Dawn and Bruce to relax into a near doze leaning their faces on the soft fur as we all rode home in silence with full tummies. The ending to a perfect day.

Before I knew it the day had come for Dawn and I to meet with Ashenee and Mary at Rose's Tea House. Even though I had been there a couple times with a lady friend I was still in aah when it came into sight just as Dawn was too. All three of them were totally enchanted just as I had been on my first visit. As Dawn said, it makes you feel as though you are stepping into another land somewhere far away.

Inside we were seated at a round table beside the window where Mary was able to have a full view of the busy street with its' many small stores lining the cleanly swept walkway. It was easy to see that both her and Ashenee were enjoying this quaint little Tea House with its' lovely servers wearing pretty floral dresses covered with a white apron of an all-over lace organdy tied in a bow at the back. Their hair was neatly pinned back with an old fashioned hair clip. A single strand of a mother of pearl necklace graced the front of their sweet-heart neckline dresses.

These servers appeared to be in their middle forties, but Ashenee whispered in a soft voice to Dawn that these old ladies looked so sweet and nice in their out-fits. Mary and I both had to suppress a smile. To us they were young.

After some deliberation, we each chose a sandwich of ham and cream cheese with sprouts on a croissant bun with a stick of crisp celery and two sweet pickles on the side. We had no trouble choosing a desert. They had a fancy layered raspberry cake with whipped cream topping. Mary and I had decided to treat our daughters just like we had dreamed of being treated by our mothers who never had the opportunity to do so.

Ashenee and Dawn both had chosen hot tea to accompany their lunch while Mary and I stuck with our tried and true coffee.

As we said our goodbyes it was bitter sweet for both Mary and I. We were happy to have had this great time together, but we both felt sad that we may not have this opportunity again. We are both aware of our deteriorating health which due to our age may not have the results we hope for. Mary said she too gets very tired and weary, but there seems to not be any reason for it. At least nothing they can put their finger on. Ashenee wants me to spend more time during the winter months with her, she said so we just may see more of each other.

Chapter Sixteen

A few days after Joe had been out doing some chores for me along with some help from Bruce I got to thinking. The siding needed to be washed as well as a repair done to the gutter on the back side. These were chores that I was not able to do by myself. Over the last few visits with Katrin and Joe we also discussed the stability of my car. I felt I could now get a car, not brand new but new off the lot due to this year's models arriving. I felt it was not fair to my family to have to come over and do these extra chores as well as worry about my car.

I loved this home where I had made many friends but with my health getting worse I decided that I would bite the bullet and move to an apartment where it would be done for me, for a price of course. Here I had enjoyed planting my flowers each spring, but that seems to be difficult in the best of days. The pruning of shrubs, mowing lawn and washing the outside of my mobile were becoming more difficult each time. I would only do this if they all thought it was a good idea. Maybe they will want me to stay here if for no other reason than to give them a little extra work. Yeah right, I laughed to myself.

Within the week, the votes were in. Fritz began it with saying yes to the car and yes to the apartment. He is the car expert in our family so I could leave that in his hands to narrow my choice down.

Joe offered to assist me with apartment hunting. A friend had suggested an apartment building next to where she lived that I might wish to check out. As it turned out it was an older building that had been well taken care of with a small unit for sale. I was not in need of anything larger, it would be too much work for me to keep clean. It was on the second floor with an elevator to assist me as well as the other owners.

With my heart pumping wildly as I hoped and prayed that my mobile home would sell quickly, it did. Before I knew it my things were settled into their new home as was I.

My new car was a robin egg blue Toyota Camry. I felt with Fritz's help I made a good deal. Fritz sold my Ford for me getting me a little more for it than a car dealer was willing to give. I felt safe and secure when I was out on the road. It would not let me down.

Soon along came Expo 86, the world's fair opening on May 2nd closing on October 13th by the Prince and Princess of Wales commemorating Vancouver's centennial changing the face of our city. The theme was transportation and communication.

Helen said she had a Season Pass too so we could take the bus and travel together. Her walking ability and stamina was much the same as mine so we would be compatible. And so we did. We found that we enjoyed visiting the same Pavilions, tasting the same foods and ending our long day about the same time.

There were pavilions featured from 54 nations as well as numerous corporations. Most Canadian provinces hosted a pavilion showing highlights from their home province. One of the most popular pavilions was the North West Territories.

Concerts were held to entertain visitors most of which were hosted by Red Robinson. Many visitors found getting their passports stamped at each pavilion a favourite souvenir. Postage stamps depicting the Canada Pavilion were 34 cents. British Columbia license plates with Expo 86 were available in blue on white as visitors from all over the world came.

Sometimes when Helen wasn't able to go I would take the bus by myself. Then I would wander around for a while stopping for a cup of hot chocolate with whipped cream and chocolate sprinkles on top. By that time it was time to meet with Katrin and Joe. After spending a couple more hours there they took me home. If I found that I was too tired to walk until they were ready to leave, I would sit on one of the many benches people watching. Very often someone else would sit down to rest engaging in a light conversation. Expo 86 was without a doubt a friendly and fun place to experience.

I now had a little further to go to the Senior Centre but ten minutes is not a big deal when one is retired. I still enjoyed being a part of this centre that worked for the community. It was a very social club that made a big difference in the lives of many people especially those with no family close at hand.

One sunny day I decided that I had some bills

to pay so would take advantage of doing some browsing in a few ladies retail shops keeping me out until late afternoon. I had stopped in at the White Spot Restaurant for a chicken lunch leaving me in no hurry for my supper.

Before going up to my suite I stopped in the lobby to retrieve my mail. There taped to my mailbox was a note to telephone Ida. Since this was not the usual day for us to telephone visit I thought I should call her promptly.

Earlier in the afternoon a lady that lives in the rooming house had come to Ida's door looking for me. Ida could not remember her name, but she got the important part of her message.

Nancy and her friend Edward had been in a terrible accident. They were both in the Vancouver General Hospital. They had been walking along on a gravel sidewalk deep in conversation when a speeding car with a young driver lost control striking the two of them. At this time no one knows if the driver had been drinking or just not paying attention or perhaps driving faster than he was experienced to do.

This had happened a week ago on a dark windy day heavy with pelting rain. I wonder how much this affected this accident. It still leaves a strange feeling with me that there are so many accidents in the city that one such as this does not warrant media attention. This is a downside of the city that I sometimes did not understand and certainly did not like.

I could hardly believe my ears when Ida said

that Nancy survived with a broken arm and back injuries after being thrown at least ten feet until she landed against a homeowners' fence.

Edward having been walking on the road side was not so lucky. His legs were both broken with one having to be amputated at the knee. The doctors said it was just a mass of bone splinters leaving them no other option. He also suffered with a broken arm as well as internal damage causing bleeding in the stomach. Edward has been placed in an induced coma in an attempt to control bleeding in the brain.

I don't remember the remainder of our conversation. It was as though I was somewhere between real life and outer space. After hanging up with promises of a call tomorrow I sank into my soft chair to try to make sense of it all. This is where I did my crocheting whether it was going to be a large doily or a small one it was something to do that kept my hands busy. Remembering the day I received the telephone call from the bank that Katrin had been in an accident the room began to turn. I had told myself that I was alone so I must remain in control. I lowered my head to my lap letting my eyes close as I tried to relax my mind. I felt my stomach roll as though I was going to vomit, but I told myself I couldn't. I needed to reach the bathroom first. I would do that. As I tried to stand my legs felt like rubber. They would not co-operate. It was a good thing I was home from work that day taking a sick day. Then my mind quickly shifted from my pain to my daughter.

Somehow I managed to pull myself through this horrible time to where I could be of help to my family. Accidents should never happen but they do. As I think back it seemed forever until Katrin came out of her coma. A day to rejoice and give thanks to our Lord for sure. Then began the long therapy of dedication and hard work. Today there is no sign of her injuries. She is bright and vibrant. The doctors feared she would be left with a permanent limp, but according to Katrin that was not going to happen. She said she waited too long to be like all the other girls. A little accident was not going to rain on her parade. It would not ruin what she had dreamed of for so long.

As soon as I got myself steady again I made myself a cup of weak tea. Not wanting to eat anything I decided that I would make do tonight with a slice of bread and strawberry jam, my favourite meal anyway. When I looked inside the refrigerator for the jam I noticed some mixed fruit waiting to be eaten. At first I thought not tonight, but then I remembered my mother's pink fruit bowl and serving dishes in my china cabinet. I really needed to have a chat with her, but since that was not possible I would use one of the delicate bowls. Perhaps I would feel like she was nearby. Why had I not thought of this before. One day this set will sit inside Katrin's china cabinet. She has admired it so many times while visiting me. Whenever I mention that it will be hers she quickly says not yet. You enjoy it mom, it is from your mother I would hear her say. I know Dawn loves to look into my china cabinet too when she visits asking where I got some of the different items. The next week it is the same again. I don't mind. It makes me feel happy to know that she is interested as well as admires the same things I do.

The next morning I got up early putting my usual itinerary aside. It kept coming back to my mind of Katrin and how Nancy had visited me at the hospital so many times each time bringing me a sandwich with her knowing that I would not have felt like making myself some lunch. She was right, I would eat when I get home which often didn't happen.

I had no idea if Nancy was able to eat but just in case I made her favourite sandwich of Kraft Cheez Whiz with Kraft Mayonnaise spread generously on the fresh white bread. Today I removed the crusts cutting her sandwich into four pieces. I also made one for me too as I planned to spend the day with my friend.

Nancy had told me that she only had one brother who now made his home in England. He had received a transfer there early in his working life. Both her parents passed away while she was in her twenties so with not having married she was basically alone.

As for Edward, he too was on his own. His wife had passed away numerous years ago. Their only son travelled to Scotland on a backpacking trip when he was young. There he met a lovely Scottish Lass that stole his heart. He soon found work there with promises to Edward that it was only for a couple years. Then they would be moving back to Vancouver. Well, one year led to the next until five had passed. Now there was a baby on the way. Of course the new Grandma did not want them to take her only grandchild to another country. With promises to write and visit as soon as possible, this became his new home as one year led to another.

Two babies later Edward decided he would have to take a trip to Scotland. He wanted to see his grandchildren before they grew up. He was also missing his son.

As he had explained it to Nancy he decided to scrape the bottom of the barrel and go. With a couple small gifts in his suitcase he set out on his first airplane ride. Arriving there late one evening weary from the long day, he found that they had forwarded his suitcase to somewhere unknown. Just where they did not know. He told Nancy that they apologized as they tried to assure him it would be found to which he would receive it in short order. They could not seem to understand that he could not wear an apology nor could he afford to purchase clothes for his ten day stay.

After spending six days wearing borrowed shirts from his son and night washing the remainder of his clothes his suitcase caught up to him in time to give his grandchildren their presents from Canada. A small consolation.

While there it slipped out off someone's lips that they married in a hurry as a wee one was well on the way. Unfortunately she was born asleep never to wake. This sweet little babe went to heaven without seeing her Canadian grandpa. Before leaving for home he visited the nearby cemetery where his granddaughter was laid to rest leaving a pink rose and a kiss from her Canadian grandpa.

Knowing in his heart that he would also be leaving the remainder of his family behind in a far-away country he boarded the airplane for the country that he called home thinking that perhaps one day he would visit again. So far this just has not happened nor does he wish to talk about it. He told Nancy that this is a hole in his heart that he knows shall never be filled.

After having ridden the bus to downtown Vancouver many times, today my mind did not focus on the evidence of a busy City life as we passed by. It all seemed to have just happened in a blur. I did not even notice the beautiful white church with its' tall steeple and stained glass windows that had always left me in aah as I watched for it to appear. To me a clean white church gave off a sense of peace and comfort.

The sky had turned to a dark grey that was sure to leave us with rain clouds later in the day. If I should get lucky the rain will hold off at least until I am on board the bus home then it will be just a few short blocks until I am home inside my comfortable apartment. However, I do need to transfer twice so maybe I shall hope for the rain to hold off until supper time. Then for my part it can water the grass all it wants.

As I entered the ward where Nancy lay displaying casts and bandages I felt a relief to see the smile in her eyes as I walked in. I pretty much had to sign my life away to get in as I was not family. I did not tell a lie but came as close as I dared.

As Nancy relayed this terrible accident to me I could see that it became more stressful but she insisted on telling me the whole story. She had only told it to a police officer, and as she said that is not the same as a friend. She needed to talk about it, and I was ready to listen for however long she needed.

She said they were heading out for dinner in China Town. They both had been wanting some good Chinese food for several weeks already. They were driving along paying close attention to the road as the traffic seemed to be a little heavier than usual when a dark blue pick-up truck sped through a red light. She said all she could remember was them both screaming before she woke up in the hospital.

After taking a little while to rest as well as gain her composure, she asked if she could talk some more. She said she felt like she needed to get it all out. Little by little Nancy told me what little she knew of Edward. As much as she begged to see him she was repeatedly told it was not possible to move either of them. Edward was in another acute care ward on another wing. They kept telling her he had not regained consciousness, but they would be sure to let her know when he does. For now he just needs to sleep, and you must not worry. Easy for them to say, but not so easy when it is your special friend.

When the nurses came in to tend to her, I said I would stretch my legs in the hall. Once there I went to the desk in hopes there would be a nurse that would be able to shed a little light on Edward if I promised not to share it with anyone including Nancy.

The kindest older nurse was just waiting to hear that. She had been speaking with the doctor as to how they would prepare her for the terrible news that lay ahead in the next day or two. She would need a friend for support since she had no family. Was there another friend besides me she asked .I explained to her that she was friendly with a lady by the name of Rita, but I would prefer to have Rita call in as I did not wish to commit her.

Nurse Margaret asked me if I would mind leaving Nancy fifteen minutes earlier to have a conversation with her in the nurses office. The doctor would be there too. At that time they would fill me in on Edward's condition.

As I stepped away I knew it was grave. Would I be able to put on a brave face for my friend for the remainder of the afternoon without giving away anything. I did not want her to be suspicious as I did not know what to say without telling her the truth. That was not my position.

As I rode the bus home during the busiest time of the day, I was so lost in my thoughts that I had not even noticed the rain falling ever so gently. By the time my neighbourhood came into view the skies were rocking with thunder banging far enough away to be safe, but still near enough to be heard. I needed to hurry.

As soon as I got myself settled with a couple crackers, a slice of cheese and a cup of hot water I began to run the unbelievable conversation over in my mind that I had had with Margaret and the doctor. It was like it was something from some weird story someone with an unsettled mind said to shock his friends on a Halloween night. I needed to call Rita.

As Margaret wasn't too sure if they would be sharing it all with Rita I just told her what they asked me to share. The rest I would need to keep to myself. I was relieved to hear Rita say that she would go to the hospital in the morning. Since she would have to leave just after lunch it would likely be enough company for Nancy for one day. They were going to be administering a heavier sedative beginning tonight. While she was sedated the doctor would explain that they would be removing all life support systems from Edward. They had received permission to do so from his son via telephone.

I could not believe just how severely he had been injured. With the severe bleeding in his brain, not to even mention in the stomach it appeared to be the kindest way. He is just existing. He will never live a life again.

Nancy is healing well. In approximately a week she shall be released. She will still require some physical therapy for the next while but will be able to live on her own.

As I lay in bed later that night my mind would

not leave the time my family experienced the terrible ordeal that Katrin went through. It seems there is always something coming along to remind me of my daughters' past trials. Perhaps this is a way of making us thankful for what we do have. Katrin was one of the blessed victims of these dreadful accidents.

Weeks had passed, the first few in a whirl until life began to settle down. Nancy was devastated to hear of Edward's passing even though she was heavily sedated. Slowly it began to sink in, her good friend would not be coming home and there was not a thing she could do for him.

Yes, Nancy will miss her good friend. Like she said she will always see his big smile as it spread across his broad face looking down at her with eyes twinkling. My dear, I am right as rain he would say. This was followed by a wink of his bright blue eyes that he thought no one saw. I did. I always thought they had deep feelings for each other, but they seemed to prefer their own space at the same time.

Each evening before I started my supper I gave Nancy a telephone call to be sure she was alright. At least as good as she could be expected to be. Depending on how chipper she sounded determined the length of the call. A few times she mentioned how she envied me having children and grandchildren to visit me leaving me with some unique memories of their visit. I just then realized how much a person without a family looses. Of course my mind went to Floyd.

I knew from Joe that he and Katrin, Dawn and Bruce had stopped by his place a couple times for a short visit on their way home from visiting Joe's parents in Manitoba. He never disclosed the nature of their visit nor did I ask I just knew that I wasn't surprised. He did say that he was doing well. He was living with his brother. Together they had a busy painting business in town.

I remember how homesick for her dad Katrin had been. Many evenings on the farm before Katrin went to bed she would snuggle with her dad as he sang You Are My Sunshine to her. This seemed to be her quiet time. Besides she was a daddy's girl. Fritz I am sure was homesick as well but was a tougher nature. Even while we lived in the North they would cry to each other but not to either Floyd or I. Sometimes it was as though they felt they only needed each other to complete their world.

When Floyd passed away Fritz and Katrin flew to Saskatchewan for his service. I do not know who it was that called them not that it matters. I was proud to know that I had raised them to be respectful caring adults. I no longer feared they would be taken anywhere they didn't wish to go. I have often felt they loved their father, as they should, but were thankful to be away from the hard meagre life that was in store for them.

Later that fall I received a telephone call from my brother Klaus. He was coming to visit for a couple days saying he just needed a couple days away from work so thought he would spend it with me mostly just talking. I was delighted but wondered just what that was about.

The day after he arrived he brought up the subject just as we finished our breakfast.

"Emma. I do not wish to hurt your feelings, but there are some things that I think you must know. I am sure it is no surprise to you that it concerns Fritz and Katrin. Since they do not wish to seem ungrateful for all that you have done for them to make their life better they said they were not willing to share the nature of Floyd's funeral with you. I think it will give your mind some peace to not spend more days wondering, and perhaps coming to the wrong conclusions. If you wish to forget these things as fast as I tell you that is fine too. I will understand."

"Klaus, I have the feeling we need to take our coffee into the living room where we can spend this time in a more comfortable chair."

And so Klaus began telling me everything he could think of. Yes, sometimes it made me feel bad, but other times I felt grateful that this is now out in the open. His story went like this taking up the whole morning.

Fritz had called him after he received a call from Floyd's brother to inform him and Katrin of the passing of their father. With the weather being as unstable as it usually is at this time of the year, he told Fritz that they should get a morning flight to Regina where he would pick them up at the airport. If they took an early flight they could be in Watrous in time for the afternoon service.

Not thinking to mention that their weatherman has been calling for snow on October 4th they both arrived wearing Sunday clothes fit for the milder coastal weather. Katrin was wearing a dress with high heeled shoes, the only pair she had with her. The closer they drove to Watrous the larger the fluffy white snow flakes came. Soon they were coming down heavier and heavier. The wind was picking up blowing them around in giant swirls.

When they arrived Klaus said they went immediately to Floyd's home where his brother was waiting for them. After saying hello he suggested that Fritz and Katrin take his car so they could go for a quiet coffee downtown by themselves to gather their thoughts.

Later Fritz told him that they stopped at a couple shops in town just to get a feel of the community their dad lived in finally locating a cafe they thought would be one that they could have that cup of coffee without peering eyes. Much to their shock as they entered the front door there was a sign posted to say this cafe would be closed for two hours in the afternoon for the funeral of Floyd Ziegler. There was also a sign folded to a standing position at the front counter for all to see as they paid their bill before leaving. This had also been the scene in each of the businesses they had previously visited.

They had no idea their father was such a popular and respected man in the community. After leaving the sandwich they purchased to share with only a couple bites taken, they drank their coffee so they could leave. They now felt all eyes were on them. They clearly stood out as two visitors to this small town.

When Fritz went up to pay leaving Katrin sitting in their booth, the waitress promptly asked him if they had come for the funeral. He quickly thought it best to be truthful so he said yes. In the usual small town way she thought nothing of asking if they were relatives to which he said that Floyd was their father. She was clearly shocked for a moment. Quickly regaining her composure she offered her condolences saying that we will see the whole town there. She then offered the shocking information that no one knew he had children.

She was right. That afternoon Watrous became a ghost town. Not a single person or vehicle was out on the streets. They were all in the Lutheran Church. There was standing room only spilling outside onto the steps. Every chair and step had been filled.

Following the service Klaus drove Fritz and Katrin to the cemetery as they both chose to not go in the black limousine reserved for family members. By this time the snow had completely covered the ground leaving no sign of the grass below its pristine blanket. The snow was coming down faster and thicker as though it was trying to keep up with the cold air. Blankets were carried to the gravesite to wrap around Fritz and Katrin. Nothing could be done for their cold wet feet. When the service was completed they stepped forward to lay the wreath of fresh flowers they had asked me to pick up for them. While Fritz had eyes filled with water, Katrin was openly weeping. Unfortunately like me they could hear some of the judgemental comments that were said not meaning to be heard so therefore should never have been uttered by even careless people. Klaus said how sad he felt for them that they were the ones to receive the blunt of the criticism.

From there they went back to the home of Wilhelm where his family were gathering. This was a very uncomfortable time for Fritz and Katrin as their cousins kept looking at them as though they were from some foreign land, clearly not one of them. I too felt they were being judged. When two cousins appearing to be in their thirties came into the kitchen displaying the fresh flowers they had returned to pick from the their wreath, it was the last straw. Katrin could take no more.

It was early evening when Klaus suggested they leave as Fritz and Katrin had a plane to catch in a few hours. They were only too eager to be on their way.

It was very apparent that Katrin did not like cold weather especially the snow, nor was she a farm girl. She was a spring and fall person. I loved spending time with her especially when she worked with the silk flowers. Her business thrived on word of mouth advertising. Sometimes she even received a request to decorate a cake for someone. Floyd would have been so proud of his children.

Fall came slowly creeping in with cooler winds and shorter days As the seasons begin to turn from one to the other I noticed how they just seemed to slide from one to the other with no drastic change unlike the North. When fall came we could go to bed one night to a brisk fall air and wake up to swirling white flakes of snow in the morning. I do miss not being able to see the silver sliver of the moon in the clear night sky or the sparkling stars in the night sky that were not hidden behind the smog that seemed to show itself so often in the city.

The colder weather also brings with it more discomfort with my arthritis. My joints have been worse than they have ever been not to mention my back. The hip replacement that I had had a few years earlier had improved my back pain tremendously. Nothing lasts forever.

I told my friends that I was going to stay with Katrin for a couple weeks. I know her and Joe thought that I needed company more than anything. After I had been there for nearly a week Katrin told me that while I had been having my afternoon nap I had received a telephone call from Mona, a lady from the Senior Centre. They were having a luncheon for some reason the following Monday. Katrin and I were invited. When she said that she was sure we would be able to come I was a little surprised but didn't question it too much. I did ask her if she was sure she was not too busy because I did not need to go. Giving me some kind of reason why she would like to go, I just left it at that thinking if she doesn't mention it again I won't either.

Monday morning came. As usual Katrin made

me a delicious bowl of hot oatmeal porridge with raisins, brown sugar and milk. I seemed to enjoy it so much more when she made it. I know I have eaten enough oatmeal in my lifetime for three people, but I never tire of it. She likes it too and so does Bruce.

I thought a few minutes later that something was strange when she said "Well, I guess we should put on our going to luncheon duds." I knew this meant she had not forgotten. We were going. I questioned her as to Dawn. Was she planning to come over this afternoon with Nicholas and Michael.

"No mom, that is tomorrow. They will come for lunch so sleep well tonight so you are ready for those little guys." We both laughed at their energy. They were a couple cute little lively characters that loved going to grandma's house.

As we drove along I commented how winter seemed to be sneaking up on us. With discussing how the leaves have left their comfy summer branches to find themselves laying half dried up on the cold wet ground we were there before I even noticed just how fast the time had gone.

By now we had to search for a parking spot as this was the busiest time of day. Low and behold there was an empty spot real close to the door. Not thinking anything of it, we both chuckled at our good fortune. Vacant spots were hard to come by, but as Katrin said she was going to jump on it. First come first served, it was hers.

When Katrin opened the door for me, it sounded like it was filled with a zillion bees each humming their own tune. We looked at each other, Katrin with a questioning look and me with a smile. I quietly said this is normal. I am not sure what she expected but all I heard was Yikes!

We were quickly ushered in to a table at the front where the ladies quickly said it was nice to see me there. I introduced my daughter as we sat down.

I whispered to Katrin, "How come we found a parking space and a chair at the front of the room?" With a shrug of her shoulders as if to say how would I know she laughed as though to say just our luck.

Before anything more could be said everyone was asked to be quiet as there was a special guest attending that has just arrived. I looked up and saw the Mayor standing there. How nice I thought, but he never attends. Always too busy to have lunch with the old people. I wonder what he wants, votes?

After thanking the group for the kind invitation he said how it was such an honour for him to present the guest of honour. Now what did he think he was I thought. Well, low and behold he looked directly at me.

"Emma, would you please join me here before your friends?" he said. With that he reached his hand out to help me forward. Along with Katrin's help I made it the few feet to the front as I heard the loudest applause ever. I turned to the group to see everyone standing as they clapped and clapped.

It was for me.

With words that I could barely hear because of being in such a high cloud he thanked me on behalf of the city for my hard work as a citizen in this lovely city. "We feel we want to present to the White Rock Senior Centre a larger cabinet, with a lock and a plaque commemorating your hard work. As the senior members enjoy their time here together the plaque with your name on it will bring them reminders of a job well done. Thank you Emma."

The applause was deafening said Katrin on our way home. I was overwhelmed with both excitement and appreciation. For a while we drove home in silence. Then Katrin said, "So mom, how does it feel to finally have reached your goal for the community?"

"I am not sure. Am I going to die Katrin?" I asked with half a smile. I was kind of joking but yet not.

"Mom. Why would you think such a thing?"

"You will see when your time comes to be a senior. They never honour anyone until after they are dead."

"Well, I think this time you made another first."

"So. Did you know about this?"

"I did, but I too wanted it to be a surprise to make it even more special."

"What if I wasn't going to go?"

"Oh. You were going." With that we both laughed as we shared the wonders of this special day.

The next day just as planned Katrin arrived with Nicholas and Michael roaring through the front door full speed shouting hi G.G., hi Grandma again and again until they were both atop me ready to give hugs. I always just loved to see them rambunctious as they were. They sure stirred up a dull house in a hurry.

Soon we were all sitting at the table enjoying pancakes topped with bananas and syrup. In what seemed like a short minute the pancakes were gobbled up leaving a sticky mess on the table covered in a plastic blue cloth that was easy for cleaning with a wet cloth. It was like a guarantee to be sticky.

As soon as the boys were busy playing with their toys that Grandma kept at her house for them, Katrin said that Ashenee had telephoned her that morning. At first I was a little surprised, but one look told me there was more to come, and I didn't feel as though it was good.

Katrin said how Ashenee asked about everyone before saying how they would like to try to meet for coffee one day soon when all their little ones have somewhere else to be for a while, like with their dads. Great idea I thought, but didn't say so.

"Mom. She also went on to say that Mary is not well. She has been feeling sick for a while not really being able to put her finger on what it was. Finally Kitche insisted she see a doctor. She said her mom has been talking to the Great Creator but was willing to see our traditional doctor. After some tests they found that her kidneys were not working well.

She needs to have lots of rest followed by regular blood tests. She is on medication and not able to travel. If things do not improve in the next while she will need dialyses."

"I suddenly feel as though the wind has just been taken from me," I said. "My dear friend is so sick and so far away. I will be sure to telephone her every once in a while. We could visit like that perhaps cheering her up just a little."

After Dawn and the boys left for home Katrin put the remainder of the things back that were not in their place. In but a couple minutes there was not a trace of two little active boys with sticky fingers having been there. Now I needed a rest.

That evening as we returned to the living room after having eaten way too much supper Katrin asked me if I was ready to telephone Mary. While my heart wanted to, my head was just too full. I needed until tomorrow to sort so many thoughts out. With my not feeling well and Mary sick I needed to decide just how much I was going to say. Somehow I felt that Dawn and Ashenee had already discussed it. Both mine and Mary's.

Even though discussing someone's health that could not possibly have a good outcome, I felt it very difficult to be attentive to the feelings of others as I still wished. Somehow I was not comfortable discussing in depth my health and the potential outcome. While everyone keeps saying just think positive it is so much harder to do when it is yourself with only you to see and feel what is going on inside of you. We are all aware that worrying before we need to is no help, but again that is easier said than done especially when it is one's own self. Then I need to remember that everyone has an opinion and insists on sharing it while they usually have never walked in that person's shoes.

Well, no point in putting off for tomorrow what I should do today. Make the call just like I need to.

After it rang for several times Mary answered the telephone much to my surprise. First in the conversation was the necessary preliminaries. You know, how the rest of our families are and so on including the weather. I told her how we were expecting another system in the next few days. With that she began to laugh. "I will just check the leaves in the front yard and I will know. Our system is so simple." Once again we chuckled as we talked of the high fandangled ways of the city life, and the plain country ways. We both agreed there were parts of both ways that we liked but for me the city outweighed the country. Mary had to agree but said she didn't have the luxury to choose. We both understood.

"So Mary. Dawn tells me she was talking to Ashenee who told her you are not feeling too well. How are those kidneys behaving these days?"

"Oh Emma. Those drat things are not doing their job. I am supposed to be taking it easy not them." Even though she laughed about it, I knew she was very worried. If I was ever in her shoes I would be too. The added problem is that as Mary said, we are not getting younger like we like to wish we were.

After explaining that her doctor does not know what has caused this problem it does explain why she had been so tired all the time for the past while. She had also added some extra pounds which she now found were from the fluid build-up.

"You know Emma. All the many times that I wished I could just lay with my feet up with no work waiting for me is now here and I don't like it. Perhaps it is because it is not my choosing which day and what time." In the sound of her voice trailing off, I detected a tear rolling down her light tan cheek. Maybe it was because there were tears dripping from my eyes threatening to spill out onto my pale face as I felt the sadness of our days ahead.

"Mary I am so sorry. I wish more than anything that I could have a magic wand to wave over our heads, but I don't. We will just have to trust that our God knows what is best for each of us. May it be not too painful."

As Dawn and Ashenee had related to her my story of my health I did not feel it was important to go over it once again. By now it was evident that we both had tears falling freely making it harder than ever to say goodbye with promises to call again.

As I heard "Please Emma, let us get to speak some more. I miss you so much my dear friend but I do feel that I will soon be joining Achak. That is just for you and I to know."

"I will not speak of our deep feelings to others. Your secret is safe with me. I wonder which one of us will get to heaven first."

"Maybe, just maybe we will see each other before we get there," said Mary in a whisper. "If not, I will look for you there."

The sound of the click as I replaced the receiver was like a gong striking the Big Ben Clock as though it gave my heart a jump start to get on with life, my life.

Every few days either Katrin or Bruce would drive me out to my place just to check on things. They knew I would feel better when I knew there was no problems to surprise me. I picked up my mail, bills, advertisings and then watered my few plants. By the time we returned I was played out. I thought I must be just getting lazy. I was so accustomed to a busy active life that this maybe was just too much of a change. With that I promised myself that I would walk a little outdoors each day if for no other reason than to get fresh air.

Every once in a while I would return to my place if for anything just to visit with Helen for a few minutes. I assured Katrin and Joe that as soon as I felt uncomfortable there I would let them know. Someone would come for me. I think it was this assurance that gave me confidence that I could handle it with such a dark cloud hanging over my heard.

I knew deep down that there had been a quiet conversation that I would not be returning to either the Orchids or the Sweet Adeline Chorus. But then I wasn't attending the Senior Centre like I had faithfully done. Everyone knew. I think that was the hardest just knowing my friends all knew and expected me to be the next one leaving this mixed up world.

I was now one of those Seniors that lived mostly with their children making their biggest outings to the doctor accompanied by a family member. For some reason I had not thought that would be me. It just hadn't crossed my mind.

Chapter Seventeen

It was the first days of December 1987 when I had just finished my breakfast of toast with strawberry jam and a cup of coffee. This was my favourite. I dearly loved fresh bread with the smell of those ripe red berries loaded on top. The doctor had told me to cut back on my toast so I decided I would just have one slice each morning. That meant I had to pile the delicious sweet jam on a little thicker. It was the only option I had.

The sound of my telephone ringing so early startled me. I quickly reached for the receiver to hear the voice of my daughter Katrin. She did not sound like anything was wrong but I had to ask anyway. I felt that I was feeling much better so planned to spend most of the time in my beautiful home.

"No mom. Nothing is wrong here. I need to go out close by your place so I thought I would pick you up. If you have nothing to do, you can ride along with me. Then we can stop someplace for lunch. How would that be?"

"That would be nice. I have a doctor's appointment at one thirty though."

"That is fine with me. I will just go with you to the doctor. He is such a nice man. Why are you going?"

I was afraid she would ask. I simply said, "I am just going back to see about the blood work I had done a couple weeks ago. Remember? You don't have to come, but if you want to you can."

I knew if I tried to discourage her she would just be more adamant about coming along. I had not said anything before that I had been feeling poorly for most of the past month already. I have had to force myself to eat, hence the blood work. I thought I had put on a good front. So I thought.

As I hurried about to get myself ready to go out, I found myself feeling more concerned at what the blood work would show. If Katrin was sitting right there, and she would be, I will not be able to hide anything. Even though she never comes out and tells me, I do know that she has phoned my doctor for an explanation of tests I have had done in the past.

Helen was the only friend that was openly aware that I was not feeling my usual self for some time. It was her that had convinced me to make a visit to my doctor way back when. One day her and I had gone to Moby Dick's restaurant for lunch. While sitting there I began to feel light headed. I forced myself to finish my last piece of fish but it was a struggle. We sat there longer than usual while I finished my glass of cool water giving me a little longer to steady my wobbly legs.

As we strolled home taking in the fresh sea air with the wind blowing off the ocean water, we watched the white caps forming and rolling towards shore. The weatherman had said on the morning news that a mild storm was to come early that evening. Another system they called it. Today the cooler air felt good. For the first time the smell of deep fried food had unsettled my stomach. Normally it made me want to lick my lips in anticipation of the delicious cod fish to come.

After a few minutes Helen asked me if I was feeling better saying she thought my colour was better. More like it normally was.

"I am just fine now. I don't know what came over me. Nothing to worry about." This I will not share with Katrin.

"Emma. I have noticed that you haven't been as perky as you usual are. It is not like you to not be jumping up looking after the rest of us. As soon as someone has that look that says they might want another piece of chocolate cake, you are the first one to say you would get it. Are you feeling more tired than usual? We are not getting younger you know."

"Well you have a point there. I was hoping you know, but now you have spoiled that." We both laughed as we kept walking.

"My dear friend. I really wish you would visit your doctor once more just to convince me that all is well. I go annually for blood work you know." If she only knew that I had not shared all with her, but I just couldn't.

After promising I would do that, I told Helen the story of my buying lard in the grocery department of Woodward's to make Pigs Ears. Again it struck me so funny that I started to laugh again.

"Whatever is that and just what happened?" she asked.

By the time I had finished telling her this story as well as answering her questions as to other foods we had on the farm we were back. Now I just had to. "Do you like Pickled Pigs Feet?"

"What! Now I know you are pulling my leg."

"No Helen. When I feel a little better I shall make some for you. I know you will really enjoy them. My kids have been asking for them anyway. First I will need to see where I can purchase the feet. The Pigs Ears are just too time consuming for me now."

Now whenever I feel like there is nothing to smile about I think of poor Helen. She didn't know what to think or expect. She was a great sport. When I made them I kept enough for her and I for a lunch. She tried them eagerly and helped herself to more with just a sprinkle of vinegar on top.

As it was kind of a blustery day out, Katrin suggested that we go for a bowl of steaming hot clam chowder soup for lunch. That sounded great. I was sure I could eat that much, but no sandwiches with it.

I tried to keep the conversation off me. As I am always interested in her silk flower business, Adoren Creations, that she ran from home I was able to chatter away not leaving an opening to discuss my doctor appointment. I did love to hear of the arrangements she had made for her customers, some for themselves and others for gifts.

Soon we were sitting in the waiting room. Now I was becoming so very nervous that there could be something wrong this time. Not just the old people stuff that we must live with and get on with life.

When the nurse called my name I nearly

jumped out of my skin. Katrin jumped up too which meant she was coming in with me. That would be that.

Eventually my doctor entered this small cold room that will in itself make you shiver. I tried my best to be calm and smiley to show that I didn't even suspect there could even be a problem.

After greeting me in his friendly way, he turned to Katrin. "Hello Katrin. Nice to meet you again. You can remain in here while I speak with your mother. We are just going to go over her test results. I will also ask a few questions.

So Emma, how are you feeling? Has your appetite returned?"

"Oh yes," I fibbed knowing they both could see right through me as I put on my bravest face.

"Well, I am not too happy with your test results. Things seem to be a little off."

"What things is that?" asked Katrin.

"Well, for starters. Her white cell count is slightly off. She is also a little anaemic. I know she has always had low iron so perhaps this could be attributed to that. Is she going home with you today Katrin?"

Before she could answer I calmly said, "No. She just come to take me to lunch today."

"That is alright mom. You might just as well come to our place today since you were going to come in a couple weeks to stay until after New Years. It will save Bruce a trip out, not that he doesn't like to drive out to get you."

"But I don't have anything ready to go yet."

"That is alright. It will just take a couple minutes for you to pack your bag. Anything you have forgotten you can come and get. Bruce will be happy for the excuse to take the car for a drive. He does love to go to your place for the cookies and pop that you so spoil him with."

Before I had a chance to say anything more my doctor started telling me what a great idea that is and how he felt it would be good for me to be closer to my family. Clearly he was on Katrin's side.

"Since it is all settled then, my nurse will give you a form to have your blood work done again in two weeks. Then you can come in to see me and we will discuss it. Katrin, speak to my nurse for an appointment that will suit you both." With that he turned and left leaving me sitting there wondering what had just happened and just what was going to happen next. I feared the big C but would not express my thoughts to anyone on that. Didn't everyone think of that first?

I loved being at Katrin's home with her family, but my staying overnight meant that Bruce needed to sleep on the couch in the basement. He was the most giving teenager a grandmother could wish for but still I did not wish to take advantage of a good thing.

Two weeks later Katrin and I were sitting in the same cold waiting room wondering what is taking the doctor so long to come in when suddenly he gave a slight rap that sounded to me like a drum going off. This time I was so nervous I couldn't conceal it. I knew they both picked up on it.

His suspicions confirmed my fear. I needed to see a cancer specialist. He said he did not know for sure, but he was suspicious so best get these tests looked at by someone in that field. He had one in mind except he was away until January 2nd, 1988. I would also need to go to the Vancouver Cancer Centre to see him. Just then a nurse came in to see if I needed to be weighed etc.

"Yes she does. Please do the necessary things. The nurse will show you where you need to go. Just stick with her Emma. Katrin can wait in here."

Now just what did he not want me to hear? In case he doesn't know, I wasn't born yesterday.

On our way back to her home I asked what all he had to say.

"Well, pretty much the same as when you were in there. He went over the changes in your test results from the last time which was why he felt there could possibly be a bigger problem. This he does not know for sure. Let us try not to worry about the worst just yet. He said there is no rush, which is a good thing, so you can enjoy the Christmas holidays as always."

Next moment she was on about supper. Whenever I was at her house for supper, she would make something that I loved but did not make for myself. Cooking for just me is not the same. I can't ever make it as good as she can.

Bruce had suggested they have liver and onions tonight. Both him and I dearly love it while the rest just like it, well maybe not Dawn. That is the one thing she really doesn't like. When Katrin makes it you can cut it with your fork. When she calls to the family she is putting the liver on, you know you had better get to the table. You wait for the liver, never the liver waits for you.

A couple days before the Christmas holidays Katrin took me back for a check up. No tests, just a conversation with an in office check up. I kept feeling more and more unsettled that all was not going to be well. That was just what it was. He wanted to be sure that I was still feeling about the same with no new troubles. Other than to say that I was feeling a little more tired, I was the same. I could sleep for a couple hours in the afternoon and then still sleep for a full night.

Next question was how was I eating. I explained how Katrin made me oatmeal porridge each morning for my breakfast to begin my day. We then spent the next few minutes talking about Nicholas and Michael as well as their excitement of Christmas coming. Unless I began to have some problems I should return directly after the holiday. Katrin can make the appointment. They would make room for me. Oh dear. That doesn't sound good.

We had a beautiful Christmas again. On Christmas Eve Dawn came with her husband and two young sons for supper. When the boys had finished their dinner, Katrin gave them each a cloth bag filled with quiet toys to take with them to service that would be starting in a short while. The church was packed. Joe was busy helping out but we all sat together. The boys were so good playing with their new gifts, an early Christmas present from Grandma and Papa.

Christmas Day we went to Dawn's place as soon as we could get ourselves ready. Joe had already taken the gifts over to place them under their tree. My great grandsons would be bouncing with excitement long before we got there. What a wonderful day it will be.

We had a wonderful routine that worked for our family. This was a time we were together and I loved every second. This year it brought back memories of Dawn's first years of preparing the Christmas turkey. She was a young bride full of eagerness and energy. I sat watching her as she prepared such a magnificent meal for us to enjoy. It brought memories back of my helping her stuff the turkey, her first time. When I explained about filling the cavity with the dry stuffing, she looked at me in shock. "Grandma! I am supposed to put my hand in there!" I couldn't stop laughing for the longest time that day. We still laugh over that one.

Since then she has become proficient in cooking these special dinners for the family. She makes her homemade cranberry sauce to accompany her perfectly roasted turkey. I honestly think she makes better stuffing than I did. A large salad accompanies the vegetables as well. Katrin brings the homemade pumpkin pie.

This year we reminded ourselves of the year as she was taking it out of their wall-mount oven she bumped the side of the oven sending the pie flying onto the floor spilling some of the filling over the side onto the dinning room carpet. As she gasped in horror, we all came running bursting into laughter. Not much filling was lost but a mess to clean up off both kitchen tile and dinning room carpet floors. After dinner we all agreed that it was the best pie she has ever made, but might not want to deliberately drop the next one.

With memories being resurfaced, I couldn't do anything but be happy forgetting my troubles if but just for these couple days. Like every other year they all spoiled me fussing over me. Most of all I enjoy just watching them all together being happy. Nicholas and Michael were growing so fast. I got to play play-doe with them building snowballs and baseball bats.

The next day, Boxing Day, was also a fun filled day. Each year Katrin and Joe with their family spent brunch with their friends. I knew them all so well too over many years. I was invited and just too happy to attend. While they took turns hosting, this year it was Katrin and Joe's turn to host.

This was another day that went by quickly not leaving me time to think of bad things to come. When I retired for the night I was tired, a happy tired, so I slept well. I always enjoyed sleeping in Bruce's bed. When I opened my eyes in the morning I would look straight ahead at the bright coloured racing stripes on the wall. It always made me smile. When Dawn was home before she married this room was filled with girly things in pink and purple. Now it was filled with wheels and motors that roared.

The time between then and January 2nd eventually passed. My mind was more and more on my problem. The day Katrin and Fritz took me into Vancouver to see the specialist I was just plain and simple worried, each and every moment. I felt it, and it was not good.

This amazing doctor had looked over the results of the many tests I had undergone before he saw me. As we sat in his office he repeated the same questions that I had already answered many times before. He said he wanted me to stay in the hospital where further testing could be done as he wanted them. This did not sound good, but stay I must.

The next day Katrin and Joe came in to see me bringing some of my comfy sleep wear with them. My own slippers. My street clothes went home with them to prevent anything getting lost. By now they had rechecked my blood work again. I knew I would soon feel like a pin cushion. I would not complain no matter what. They were doing their best for me.

I was placed in a semi-private room with a delightful Chinese lady. She spoke very little English but we managed to converse for the amount either of us felt up to it. Each Dawn came with Nicholas and Michael Mrs. Ng would call them over beside her bed sharing smiles as she reached her arms out to them. Then she opened her night table taking out two large bright shiny oranges handing them each one. In China oranges represent good luck and wealth. If a few day passed without their visit Mrs. Ng was sure to ask for them. She loved seeing them as much as I did. They always made us smile leaving behind a happier atmosphere in our room.

As I was having pain in my lower back they were giving me a light dose of morphine which if nothing else made my head foggy. At that time I asked for the doctor.

"What is it Emma? Are you not comfortable while we do these tests?"

"I am fine with that. Everyone here looks after me just fine. That is not what I want to talk to you about. From here on I want to turn over my care to Katrin. Please do not try to explain this all to me. It just seems too much for me to grasp. She should have the last word in my medications. I have already asked her to keep me comfortable. Do what needs to be done to extend my life but nothing to prolong my death."

It was not long before my daughter quietly stepped into my room. Katrin, I said, I do not feel well enough to continue my story for you but then you already know it. Please take the time from your busy life to share mine with Nicholas and Michael. You will need to write it down. I would like them to know who I was, not just a name in the family tree. Be sure to tell them how I loved to see their bubbly faces full of energy and love. Their hugs and kisses have been so special.

When I spoke to the doctor this morning, I asked him to hand over my care to you. With the medication he gives me I feel like my head is full of feathers, my eyes do not want to stay open for very long, and my legs are wobbly when I walk which isn't very far. Please do not let them keep me on life support. That is not living. Sometimes they just wish to prolong death. Mine is going to come before my next birthday, that he has told me. No one can stop it.

I have told him that my wish is to die in comfort with as little pain as possible. If you feel I need more medication please say so. Work it out with the doctor. I do not wish to be one of those patients that is disturbing the others because I am not comfortable. I will try to not be miserable to the staff. I would like Nicholas and Michael to still visit me. I look forward to their fun visits. This place needs a little life. In short do not forget about me here. Keep me in comfort care.

Over this period of time I, Katrin, tried to answer any questions she posed to me as to what I remember as well as my feelings. There weren't many questions on her behalf regarding this. I chose instead to talk of some of the fun times and silly things that happened being careful not to upset her as I was aware of the most likely prognosis. I chose to not bring up when times were tough here in the city, but rather some of the interesting things we did.

I did not dwell on it but casually mentioned one day that it would have been better for both Fritz and I had we been told straight up what her plans were. I expressed how I knew it didn't always work out the way she thought it would which I now can understand, but most of it did. On the whole it was for the better for us all. We still missed and loved our dad. There I ended that subject. I felt sure she did not need anyone to tell her that.

I did not mention that I did not like Jack or that I was happy to see him go. I never mentioned that I knew he had taken advantage of her because I was sure she already knew these things. She did not need to hear that again either.

Perhaps we spent most of our reminiscing on her times while she lived in the mobile home which of course led to the usual story when Bruce soaked her with the garden hose. I thought she needed something to laugh about. That night I asked him if he could tell me just how it went as mother cannot remember it all. She does remember how she had to completely change clothes. She said her face was so soaked she couldn't see out of her glasses. I would like to write it down and then read it to her. Here is what he told me.

I was about seventeen because I drove out to grandmas house to clean her gutters. I was standing on the ladder washing her gutters out with the garden hose. You know how she always had to be right there watching what you were doing. She was standing right beside that big raspberry bush she had in her side yard. Anyhow, I had the hose nozzle hooked on to the gutter as I climbed down the ladder to move it over. I guess I bumped the hose off the ladder and it fell down onto the grass landing on the handle sticking it in the on position. The funny part was that it was pointed right at her head and hit her in the face. The cold wa-

ter wouldn't stop spraying. hahaha I was laughing pretty hard so I don't remember much after that but she got pretty soaked. good times.

Epilogue

It was nearly a week after her admittance to the Vancouver General Hospital that the doctor explained to her and myself the extent of her illness as tactfully as possible. When he was finished he asked me to go home for the night. I could return the next day in late morning. As much as I hated to leave I knew my mother would rather have alone time where she would not have to hide her feelings which I knew was going to be devastating. When she told me she would be alright I didn't for a moment believe it, but she needed her dignity in tact.

On my long drive home through the busy city traffic I wondered how she could possibly handle anything so devastating. I shall always remember her saying to him, "So next month I shall celebrate my birthday in here, but I will not celebrate the next birthday."

"Yes Emma, I am afraid that is the way it appears."

This is something that I have read in books, it does not happen to my own mother. She was a good mother. She sacrificed so much to do what she felt was the best for Fritz and I. Yes, she made mistakes along her journey, but so have we all. We do not have the opportunity to walk our busy path after a rehearsal. We all must do the best we can. She did. The only way it could have been better in my eyes is if dad could have, and would have, walked it with her. They both had their reasons for making their choices. That I accept.

After the initial shock that I am sure she thought would come but of course hoped beyond hope it wouldn't, she began to settle into herself. She looked forward to being released. Even though she always said I was not to take her to live with us, even if she asked because she felt it was too much for a family, suddenly it hit her. This was real. This was happening to her, now. She knew she was all alone.

I didn't ask her if she wanted to. The doctor and I just told her that when she was released she would be living with Joe and I. She would see my family doctor who would then report to him. My poor mother. I don't know how she could even begin to grasp this devastating news but she seemed to, at least a little.

Two days before that was going to happen she telephoned me. She sounded elated. She had some good news for me. I held my breath. I had not received a call from the doctor that there had been any change to her condition. Her excitement still rang in the air.

In an excited voice Mother said to me, "This morning a nurse came in to see me. Tomorrow I am going to have a small surgery. They will remove the tumour and then I can go home to my own home. I will be cured. Isn't that wonderful?" She had not sounded this happy for I don't know how long, and now the doctor and I will need to once again explain the terrible truth.

I was speechless. I did not know what to say. There was no way I knew this could be as her doctor had not telephoned me first as he said he would. I did not want to put a cloud over her rainbow so I tried to be ever so careful with what I said. It was only for a doctor to speak to a patient on such serious matters not the nurse or family. I knew she was waiting for me to rejoice with her. I couldn't lie to her.

Finally, as calmly as I could I said, "I am just about ready to come to see you so we shall talk then. Ok?" I had to get off the line. I was shaking.

Immediately I called her doctor explaining to his nurse why I needed to speak with him before I left. After leaving me on hold for only a couple minutes she told me that he would meet me at the hospital in forty five minutes near the nurses station. I would need to hurry. I now had a bit of a drive through the city. Oh please God. Let rush hour be over.

This was the morning that I was kind of slow at getting things done. With the hospital trips many things at home were left to get done whenever, like this morning. Our breakfast dishes were still on the counter and I was in my housecoat and pyjamas. One look at the kitchen and I knew it had to wait once more. This is not how I would ever leave my house but Mother was in dire need of my time. I jumped into the first street clothes I could see in our closet, ran a comb through my hair, grabbed my purse and headed for the door. Oops shoes, my comfy slippers won't do Oh, how I wish.

When I arrived he explained that he had already spoken with my mother. A nurse had made a grave mistake. She had the wrong patient. Secondly that is something that a nurse should never discuss with a patient. After apologizing to me, he said he had given my mother a sedative. She would need to sleep for a while. Off to the cafeteria I went again to wait some more. My schedule had been so upset that I didn't know what I wanted or needed. Coffee was not it. I had eaten enough muffins to turn me into a doughboy so I sat with another glass of water staring at it. Maybe something delicious will appear like a fresh bowl of fruit. Not a brown spotted soft banana.

It seemed that from then on when the nurses saw me coming they were on their best behaviour. I could feel the tension. It was clear that I had gone straight to the boss, and they did not like it. They were in trouble. If we don't look out for our family who will? What would they have done if it was their mother? I wanted to ask them if they would want this for their loved ones but knew I shouldn't. I felt like I was beginning to unravel. I couldn't.

The day came that she was to be transferred to Surrey Memorial Hospital near where I live. She would now be seeing my family doctor. When the time came the ambulance had been needed for an urgent call. She would need to wait a little longer. While she was naturally disappointed she knew there was someone in need of care that she was already receiving. She just looked up at me saying, "It is alright dear. There is someone that is sicker than I. My turn will come." With that she turned on her side closing her eyes. I knew she wished to talk to no one.

The next day following I received another call from Mother before I was ready to leave. That was actually the day I was not going to go up until Joe came from work. We would travel this forty five minute drive together, one car and time for conversation before we became exhausted again. She was upset. The nurse told her when I got there I would be taking her in my car to Surrey. As gently as I could I said she should just not say anything to them that wasn't necessary. I will be there as soon as I can. A call to Joe and I was off.

As I passed the nurses desk I kept my eyes to the floor fully aware that they had something to say to me. For now I put them on ignore, but the fire in their eyes were boring holes in me.

When I peeked into mother's room she was laying on her side facing the far side so I tip-toed over to the other side of her bed thinking she must be asleep. Slowly her eye-lids began to open with a smile on her face. Just like a kid having pulled one over on someone she said she was pretending to be asleep. I had to laugh with her. Apparently it worked. She was getting good at this little game, and enjoying it too.

Once again I went over it with her how I had not heard from the specialist so therefore she was not going anywhere. Then I reminded her that the nurses do not have the authority to discharge a patient, your clothes are at home and I am not taking you.

After a quick smile she told me how the lady

that had been beside her had been sent home in a taxi the previous night. I couldn't believe that she was actually discharged. She did in no way seem to be near well enough. Maybe Mother missed something like just where it was taking her. All the same it was very unsettling. Today she had a new roommate. One that was loud and complaining.

Soon a nurse entered asking me to come to the desk. I knew what was coming. Another told me how they needed her bed for another patient, which I am sure they did, so I needed to take her home today. The doctors just don't understand.

After taking a couple breaths I said, "I do know there are many people needing beds. How much sicker can one be than to be dying? Two doctors have told me she will be here until there is a bed available in Surrey Memorial where her new doctor can observe her for two days before discharging her." With that I turned and walked away. I had to before I said something that was rude or regrettable.

I too was in a hurry for her to be transferred. It seemed that each new day brought a new challenge with the nurses. By now Mother was a pro at pretending to be sleeping. My friends Sarah and George lived closer to Vancouver. George would often stop in to visit her on his way home from work. It became a standing joke that when he came home Sarah would phone to say "Well, she is still there according to George." Mother loved his visits. They were not long but he always straightened the blankets before leaving.

Finally she was moved. Not just was it a fifteen minute drive but she was that much closer to coming home, our home. At least she could have some happiness before it became unbearable where she would need to return.

After she was discharged she needed to go to the Cancer Centre in Vancouver each week. There they took blood samples and asked her how she was. For these trips Fritz drove picking mother and I up on the way. The trips were hard on her. The bumps in the road irritated her back. The good part was the new scenery as we drove in and out. The other bad part was each trip she had to see the young people hanging around waiting for their turn to have blood work done for the same reason. Finally one day she said to us, "I am not going back."

Fritz and I just looked at each other for a moment. Now what. "So mom, I think Dr. Yeung might need the blood tests in order to prescribe your pain meds. How about if Katrin speaks to him before making such a big decision," said Fritz.

"I will ask him if it is still necessary or if there is some other way we can do this. Would you like to go with me to his office? It is only a few blocks away," I said.

"No. Please do it for me. I find it so depressing and confuses my mind."

Well the next day his nurse phones to see if we are home. Dr. Yeung would like to stop in for a few minutes. I was elated. The timing could not have been better.

After a couple minutes of friendly questions

he said he had something to suggest. "If it was alright with you Mrs. Ziegler I would have your tests done in Surrey and they could forward the results to Vancouver." Can you believe it? There are times that things just have a way of working out. He felt the drive was too long. Finally just a tiny bit of good news. The bad news was that the prognosis was no better.

Dr. Yeung had a shocked look on his face when she said, "You know. Katrin gets me dressed. Fritz helps me into the car, then into the wheelchair to wheel me upstairs for my blood work. They ask me a couple questions. Then its, yes Mrs. Ziegler you still have cancer. Sorry we can't do anything more for you. Then its the reverse trip home. Then I am so tired I can hardly eat my supper. What is the point? I was going to tell you I am not doing that anymore." Now Fritz and I knew it was also because she just couldn't bear to see all the young people suffer any longer, but did not wish to relay this to Dr. Yeung in front of her.

For the most part the next while was uneventful. Some relatives and some friends dropped in to see her for a short visit. While they were over, it cheered her up, but when the time came to say good-by it was dreadfully hard. She then retreated to her bed to weep alone. Sunday afternoons we tried to take her out for an ice cream treat. Someplace not too far away. Whatever she thought she would like we got it.

As sick as she was each morning without fail after eating her breakfast and settling into Joe's big chair she faithfully thanked me for getting her dressed and making breakfast for her. I made the best porridge she would say. It seemed that each small thing I did, each meal I made she was sure to extend a special thank you saying how much she appreciated it. It made my extra work worthwhile. Her true caring heart was showing every day.

She would still ask where Dawn and those little boys were if they missed more than two days. Dawn often made a fresh chocolate pudding, Mother's favourite, to bring along for an afternoon treat. I usually had her other favourite on hand, cookies. Mother thought they were a staple in her life now. For years she always had homemade cookies filling a special large cookie tin ready to go. It rode everywhere in the car with her always sharing with her passengers.

Little by little we could see her fading, ounce by ounce, inch by inch. It was evident that her pain was increasing, but she never complained. I noticed the first big change when she asked me one day if she had to get changed or could she spend the day in her nightgown and housecoat. Of course she could. I suggested she let me know when she felt up to changing. While she agreed unless we were going for ice cream in the afternoon she did not wish to change. She was noticeably more tired. I suspected her pain was getting stronger. She was spending less time watching me do the things I needed to do. That was so unlike her.

During that summer Joe and I decided to paint the outside of the house. \We were home anyway and true to form she wanted to sit outside and watch us. So when the sun shone Mother was there to enjoy it. She always enjoyed being right there to see what was happening whenever we were doing something. It seemed to have given her an added distraction. Unfortunately, the painting was done, so was she.

It was when the air began to cool preparing for the fall to arrive. Leaves were falling covering the ground below, the sky was often darker making the days not so enticing to go outdoors. As long as I can remember Mother had a saying that when the leaves fall, so do the people. I tried to stay away from that part of the fall weather. She did too, but I knew what was going through her mind.

Along came September as well as the more evident change in her health. The blood tests were now being done at home, an in home service for those that were just not able to get to the lab. Dr. Yeung said it had now become too much for her.

Just when I thought it was about time that I receive a telephone call from him regarding the last test his nurse telephoned. If we were to be home Dr. Yeung would like to stop by after his office hours. I thought how fortunate we were to only be about six blocks away with a caring doctor that was just too happy to care for his patients. I thought sometimes that we got a little extra as I remembered the day when Bruce was about seven, he stopped by the house for some reason. Before he left he gave Bruce a ride in his new vehicle turning into a hero for life.

As I suspected it was not good news once again. As soon as there was an empty bed she needed to be moved into the hospital where she would be able to have continuous medical care. She now needed to receive morphine to keep the pain under control. I could not administer that. Now we wait again for a bed. He anticipated that she would travel by ambulance once again. Now Mother spoke up in her now weakened voice.

"Thank you Dr. but it is only a mile away. Katrin can drive me in her car. She is a good driver you know. There are too many people waiting for that ambulance. I will not tie up the ambulance when it is not that necessary."

With a smirk on his face he knew her mind was made up. She really was once again thinking of others.

"Katrin. I will let you know when I get her admitted from here. Then you will need to take her over right away so her bed doesn't get taken by someone coming in by ambulance. Ok Mrs. Ziegler?"

"She will be ready, won't you mom?"

Mother just nodded. I knew what she was thinking, but I could no longer keep her pain under control with over the counter meds. I too knew that so many times when a patient returns to the hospital in this condition they will not return home. I am not sure who felt worse, but I was the one that had to make like it was alright. That would not happen to my mother. She would be an exception.

The next morning the call came. We needed to

hurry. I am not sure which of the many incidents was the worst, but this was in the list. Mother tried to be brave making it seem like it was just another outing. As we left the house I saw her take a final look back at each room as we walked out our cedar door to the carport where my brown Chevy waited. I felt as though I was taking her to her death bed.

Her room was a nice bright room to be shared with another lady. They soon made a friendship which I am sure was bonded with the same terrible dreaded disease. I was so grateful that her roommate was a quiet considerate lady. They would be a comfort to each other in their own way.

Fritz and Stacey were as always regular visitors. This was a time that I would not need to be there. Most times I didn't know just what I needed or wanted to do with this free time, my life was a daze.

Once again Dr. Yeung reminded me that Dawn should bring Nicholas and Michael for regular visits. Everyone looked forward to seeing them including the nurses and most of all Mother. Dawn continued to bring her homemade chocolate pudding for a treat eventually needing to assist with the spoon. Bruce continued to come on his motorcycle with a single rose safely tucked inside his jacket protected from the nasty weather. The nurses had a bud vase just waiting.

As each day dragged on Mother seemed to fade some more not wishing to take in much conversation. I didn't know what to do to help make her more comfortable so with the approval of the staff,

I purchased a Lamb Skin Blanket for her to lay on. She said it felt lovely, her favourite word. I hoped it would prevent bed sores as she was not getting up to walk very much.

One day when I was there I felt that there was something she wanted to say so I just asked her.

"Well, neither of us want to complain for fear we will put the nurses against us, but we have both asked for strawberry jam for breakfast. All we ever get is marmalade or grape jam."

After thinking on it for a moment, I said "Mother. I have an idea."

I walked straight over to the kitchen opening the frig door. With a quick scan I spotted a large foil baking pan with jam in it. With only a glance I noticed that there was another pan below it. I had to look. Just as I suspected there was the strawberry jam with the marmalade and grape on top. Mother and Ina would have strawberry jam, and as much as they wanted.

First I peeked into their room to be sure there were no nurses attending. Back I went filling my hands with the coveted jam. As I walked in I motioned for them to not say a word. Two smiles greeted me.

First I placed some in the top drawer of my mother's night stand laying a serviette over the top to conceal her stash. Once more I put my finger to my lips. I had to do the same for Ina before anyone came. Then I whispered to each that tomorrow I would bring a better cover. They should take the strawberry and replace it with the unwanted. I would move it to the kitchen when I come. And so this became our little game each day. They were both like two little girls that had just found a cookie in the cookie jar. As far as I know no one else knew our secret.

Several days later I got to thinking how when I filled out the menus for the following day I would circle buttermilk as they both loved it. For what reason I don't know, I asked them if they were getting tired of it. I knew from the look on both their faces something was amiss. Off to the kitchen once more but there was no evidence of such a stash. That wasn't the problem.

They had not been given it even though it was on their menu. So off to the desk I went to see if it was still available. Hesitantly a nurse said yes.

"That's good to know. Since there is so much they are no longer able to enjoy it is nice to know that they can have this little treat each morning. It is also healthy for them. They will be excited when I tell them what will be on their breakfast trays. Thank you." The guilty faces could not hide the truth. The next day things changed. Buttermilk it was for both.

Her days were pretty routine as they are for patients. As long as I left my red jacket on the spare chair she knew I was somewhere nearby. One afternoon I noticed a couple walking back and forth looking into the rooms. Finally I stood up asking them if they were looking for someone special.

"Yes. We are looking for a Mrs. Ziegler."

Mother was sitting up on the side of her bed

when she heard this familiar voice. She turned to the door just in time to see their mouths drop open. They were close friends from the Senior Centre. Later they apologized to me that they had not recognized her. I was not surprised. There were times when I hardly did myself, and I very seldom missed a day.

It was just the middle of November when Mother had taken a much greater turn. She was barely eating or drinking. Walks were a thing of the past. She no longer looked forward to company other than family. Along with Fritz and Stacey we tried to cover her days and evenings so she would not be alone. My friends Sarah and George came by as often as they felt they should and could. She had stopped crocheting about a month ago due to lack of interest and energy. Her stash of strawberry jam was no longer disappearing. She did try to eat a little oatmeal in the mornings with pudding cups throughout the day. They needed Dawn to show them how to make good pudding so she said.

A month had gone by since Halloween trick or treating was just hours away. Nicholas and Michael had come to show off their costumes to their great grandmother. I had left home early in the morning planning to return before four o'clock to prepare my treats. I did not like to be on the road when the children were running all over the place. As we always had at least a hundred children driving was dangerous. As I neared her room I could hear her moaning. This did not sound like comfort care to me. Just as I feared she was tossing in pain. Promising my mother that I would speak to the nurse I laid my jacket on the chair beside her bed before leaving the room.

It seemed to take much coaxing to get the nurse to agree to an increase in her meds. If she could just wait a little longer she will get some she kept repeating. Then she would tell me how she is on a schedule. Finally after what seemed to be a stressful conversation she agreed, but I was fearful this would only be while I was there. I knew we were in for a long night.

As soon as my mother had settled down after my promising I wouldn't leave, I found a pay phone so I could place a call to the doctors office. After leaving the information with a nurse I returned to settle into the big uncomfortable green chair. Treats were not going to happen this year.

With her medication having being strengthened she seemed to be in less distress for the next few weeks. While she slept a lot, she did wake to speak with family. Her eating had waned even more. She did not need to be weighed to see that she had lost more weight. It was as though this terrible disease was eating her up.

The end of November had now come. As I stepped off the elevator from the far end of the hall, I heard the eerie screams of someone in extreme pain. The closer I got I knew in my gut and heart that it was my very own mother, the one who had quietly bore her pain for so long.

I took off in a run to find her wreathing in pain with poor Ina laying in the next bed trying to utter comfort, but being too weak herself to speak loud enough to be heard. I tried to comfort her as I assured her I was there, Halloween had long been forgotten. I had heard that pancreatic cancer was the most painful of all. I could see why.

As Mother clutched her stomach in tears and screams she begged me to make it stop. She said they won't give me any more medication. Please dear, get me more she begged. Then she said something that I thought hit the nail on the head. "They would not let their dog die like this."

I quickly kissed her forehead promising I would be back as quickly as I could leaving my coat in the chair for reassurance. When my back was to the room I broke into a full run all the way to the nurses desk not caring that people that could see me were saying I shouldn't be running.

Immediately I asked for the head nurse to which I was told she was busy. "No. I need her now!" This was the first time I had raised my voice to a staff member that I always felt was doing their best. Suddenly she appeared looking at me like there couldn't possibly be a thing wrong.

"My mother needs more pain medication right now. Please."

"She is not ready for any more for another twenty minutes."

"Can you not hear her screaming?" With that I repeated what Mother had said as she listened with her face becoming more red by the moment.

"If I give her more now you will not be able to visit with her. I suggest you wait it out."

"What? You tell me how I can visit with her in this terrible condition. This is not comfort care. I insist you administer some right now or I will phone the doctor. Where is your mother?"

"Well, if that is what you want," as she turned from me.

It was only a few minutes later that my mother fell into a sleep rarely waking for the odd second again. It was December 4th that Bruce stopped by to see her on his way home from work. As he stood at the foot of the bed, she feebly asked who that was. Then she asked for him to come closer as she tried to lift her hand for him falling into a sleep not to awake again.

As we stayed longer with her each day, December 7th came. My friend Sarah arrived early to go to the hospital with me. As we were walking out the front door my phone rang. You need to come real soon. A quick call to Fritz and we were on our way with Sarah driving. Then we were running.

With the three of us at her side Mother closed her eyes that for the briefest of seconds had fluttered open, taking her final breath as her spirit soared to her final resting place in Heaven with Jesus.

Mother is now at peace.

Acknowledgements

To my husband Bob. Your many hours of computer assistance made this dream of sixty years possible. For me to learn the computer language at this age was difficult to say the least, but you stuck with me as you gritted your teeth wondering how this could be so hard while other times just smiling. We made it. Thank you hubby for taking the picture of the rooming house shown on the cover as well as my bio picture.

To my son Warren (Bruce) for setting up my web pages with your awesome computer skills. Your creative mind is a talent, usually. You are right, Bruce was a great guy to know, and still is. Your Grandma Frey (Emma) thought so as well as you happily gave your teenage time to her. She loved your fun times together leaving her with more laughs than tears. She loved you dearly.

To my daughter Lori (Dawn). Thank you so much for your encouragement, and sharing your ability to read for me. You too have helped make my dream come true. No matter how busy your life was with working and raising two boys, you happily made time to visit and help care for your Grandma Frey (Emma). You left a soft spot in her heart while inheriting her love to sing. She loved you dearly.

To my father Raphael (Floyd) for giving me a childhood filled with a father's love and infinite patience. As we only had one towel, on bath days you used a towel that was already wet after being used by three people with never a complaint. Many times I heard you say it was alright, I don't mind, "My kinner go first." These memories will always be with me.

I know that most of the troubles between you and my mother were due to exhaustion from the long hard days as well as being unbearably poor. There seemed to be no end in sight. I am sure there were days that neither of you thought you could pull through to see the next. My wish would have been for a better end for you. One that could have included me. I take comfort knowing you too had found a new way in this rough world that gave you some peace. I carry your love each day in my heart. Enjoy your much earned rest while you keep playing that fiddle.

Other Books by
Doreen Brust Johnson

Momma, Momma, the Preachers' Comin

Sounds in my Shadow

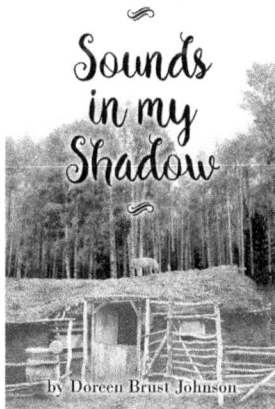

Rivershore Books

Our Young Authors Program is designed to give authors a first step into the world of publishing. We hope to encourage young authors to continue to pursue more professional publishing options as their writing and their dreams grow.

ya.rivershorebooks.com

For authors who are ready to take the next step, we also offer professional publishing options:

www.rivershorebooks.com

www.ingramcontent.com/pod-product-compliance
Lightning Source LLC
LaVergne TN
LVHW041211080426
835508LV00011B/899